DIVINE MOTHER DURGA

UNVEILING THE MYSTERIES AND SIGNIFICANCE OF NAVRATRAS

ANITA VIJ

Contents

Prologue — vii

Purpose of Writing — ix

Durga's Teachings and Stories — xiii

Empowerment and Strength — xv

Balancing Multiple Roles — xvii

Compassion and Wisdom — xix

Self-Respect and Dignity — xxi

Spiritual Connection and Inner Peace — xxiii

Role Models and Mentors — xxv

My Real Life Story: A Divine Blessing — xxvii

1. Significance Of Durga Maa — 1

2. The Mythology And Legends Of Durga Maa — 9

3. Interesting Stories And Legends Associated With Durga Maa — 17

4. The Iconography And Attributes Of Durga Maa — 24

5. The Significance Of Navratras — 29

6. Historical Context — 36

7. Spiritual Practices During Navratri — 51

8. The Nine Days Of Navratri In Detail — 56

9. Reflection On Navratras — 115

10. Continuing The Tradition — 116

11. Inspiration For Modern Lives — 117

12. A Call To Action — 118

13. Closing Thoughts — 119

14. Durga Chalisa — 120

15. Ambe Ji Ki Arti — 123

Contents

About The Author   125

Prologue

In the tapestry of life, we all strive for happiness, yet many of us find that true, enduring joy eludes us. I have walked the path of success, tasted the bitterness of failure, and learned invaluable lessons from life's struggles. Yet, despite these experiences, there remained a void, an insatiable yearning for something more profound and fulfilling. In my search for this elusive happiness, I turned inward, reflecting on my life and the essence of true contentment. It was during this introspective journey that I discovered a source of unparalleled joy: sharing the timeless wisdom and stories of our rich cultural and religious heritage.

My first endeavor was a book on Hanumanji. As I delved into the stories of the devoted monkey god, I experienced an indescribable sense of fulfillment. Writing this book not only brought me immense personal joy but also allowed me to contribute something valuable to our community. The response from readers, especially the younger generation, was overwhelming. Encouraged by this, I ventured to write about Lord Vishnu. Immersing myself in the divine tales and myths surrounding Vishnu, I found a deeper connection to my roots and a renewed sense of purpose.

Through these writings, I realized that my true calling is to preserve and propagate the knowledge of our ancient traditions, ensuring they are not lost to time, particularly for those children who grow up in foreign lands, away from the cultural heartland of their ancestors. These children, and indeed many adults, often lack direct access to the rich tapestry of our mythology, history and traditions. It is my hope that through my books, they can reconnect with their heritage, find inspiration in the real stories of our deities, and carry forward the legacy of our culture.

Now, my journey brings me to one of our most revered and beloved deities: Durga Maa. The festival of Navratras, celebrated with fervor and devotion, holds a special place in the hearts of millions. Yet, many of us are unaware of the profound significance and stories behind this vibrant celebration. Who is Durga Maa? Why do we celebrate Navratras? What are the stories behind the nine forms of the goddess, and what do they symbolize? These are the questions I aim to answer in this book.

Navratras is more than just a festival; it is a spiritual journey, a celebration of the divine feminine power that embodies strength, compassion, and wisdom. Each day of Navratras is dedicated to a different form of Durga Maa, each with its unique story, significance, and rituals. Through this book, I hope to unravel these mysteries, offering readers a comprehensive and engaging guide to understanding and celebrating Navratras with deeper awareness and devotion.

As you embark on this journey with me, I invite you to explore the divine stories, immerse yourself in the rituals, and embrace the spiritual significance of Durga Maa and Navratras. May this book be a beacon of knowledge and inspiration, helping you connect with your heritage, and find joy and fulfillment in the rich traditions of our culture.

Welcome to the world of Durga Maa and Navratras. Let us begin this sacred journey together.

Purpose Of Writing

The primary purpose of writing this book is to educate and inspire. By compiling the stories, rituals, and significance of Durga Maa and Navratras, I hope to preserve and spread the knowledge of our rich cultural heritage. This is especially crucial for the younger generation, particularly those who are growing up in foreign lands and may not have direct access to these traditions. By understanding the essence of Navratras and the divine forms of Durga Maa, readers can connect more deeply with their roots and celebrate these festivals with greater awareness and reverence.

Literary Contribution

- **Expanding Literature**: Adds to the body of literature on Hindu mythology, spirituality, and cultural practices.

- **Creative Expression**: Provides a platform for creative expression through storytelling, poetry, and reflections.

Celebrating Feminine Divinity

- **Empowerment**: Highlights the strength and empowerment represented by Durga Maa, serving as a source of inspiration for women.

- **Divine Feminine**: Celebrates the concept of the divine feminine in Hinduism and its relevance in contemporary times.

Addressing Contemporary Issues

- **Modern Relevance**: Explores how the teachings and stories of Durga Maa can be applied to address modern-day challenges and issues.

- **Cultural Adaptation:** Discusses how ancient traditions can be adapted and remain relevant in today's world.

- **Guide for Devotees:** Serves as a devotional guide for those who wish to deepen their worship and understanding of Durga Maa.

- **Navratras Observance:** Provides practical information for observing Navratras, including rituals, prayers, and fasting guidelines.

The origins of Navratri

The origins of Navratri are deeply rooted in ancient Hindu mythology and tradition, making it difficult to pinpoint an exact historical starting point. However, there are several myths and legends associated with the inception of this festival:

1. Mythological Origins:

- **Slaying of Mahishasura:** One of the most popular legends is the story of the demon Mahishasura, who was granted a boon that he could not be killed by any man or god. To save the world from his tyranny, the gods combined their powers to create Goddess Durga, who fought and eventually defeated Mahishasura after nine days of battle. This victory is celebrated as Navratri.

- **Rama and Ravana:** Another legend ties Navratri to the Ramayana. Lord Rama worshipped Goddess Durga for nine days to gain her blessings before fighting Ravana. On the tenth day, known as Dussehra, Rama defeated Ravana. This story emphasizes the triumph of good over evil.

2. Historical and Cultural Context:

- **Ancient Civilizations:** The practice of worshiping female deities can be traced back to ancient civilizations in the Indian subcontinent, including the Indus Valley Civilization, which dates back to around 3300–1300 BCE. Figurines and artifacts suggest the worship of a mother goddess, indicating early reverence for feminine divine power.

- **Vedic Period:** During the Vedic period (1500–500 BCE), rituals and hymns dedicated to female deities were prevalent. The concept of Shakti, the divine feminine energy, became more defined and integrated into Hindu practices.

3. Regional Variations:

- **In North India:** The Navratri celebrated here is closely linked with the worship of Goddess Durga in her nine forms and the triumph of Rama over Ravana.

- **In West Bengal and Eastern India:** Known as Durga Puja, this variation focuses on the victory of Durga over Mahishasura and involves grand celebrations, particularly in Bengal.

- **In Gujarat and Western India:** Navratri is synonymous with Garba and Dandiya Raas, traditional dances that honor the goddess and celebrate community and cultural heritage.

While it is challenging to determine the precise historical moment when Navratri started, it is clear that the festival has ancient roots deeply embedded in Hindu mythology and cultural traditions. The stories of Mahishasura and Rama, along with archaeological and historical evidence, suggest that the worship of the divine feminine and the celebration of Navratri have been integral to Indian culture for millennia.

Relevance of Durga's Teachings and Stories in the Lives of Modern Women

In today's world, women continue to break barriers, achieve new heights, and challenge societal norms. Amidst these advancements, the teachings and stories of Durga Maa offer timeless lessons and inspiration that are profoundly relevant to the lives of modern women. Durga Maa, with her myriad forms and attributes, embodies the essence of feminine strength, resilience, and wisdom. Her stories are not just ancient myths but powerful narratives that resonate deeply with the experiences and aspirations of women today.

Empowerment And Strength

Durga Maa is often depicted as a warrior goddess, fearlessly battling and defeating powerful demons like Mahishasura. This imagery serves as a potent symbol of empowerment for modern women, reminding them of their inner strength and capability to overcome any challenge. In a world where women often face discrimination, inequality, and various forms of oppression, the story of Durga Maa stands as a beacon of hope and courage. It encourages women to stand up for themselves, to fight against injustice, and to believe in their power to make a difference.

Balancing Multiple Roles

One of the most remarkable aspects of Durga Maa is her ability to embody multiple roles effortlessly—she is a warrior, a mother, a nurturer, and a protector. This multifaceted nature reflects the lives of many modern women who juggle various responsibilities, from professional careers to family obligations. Durga Maa's example teaches women the importance of balance and the strength that lies in versatility. It inspires them to embrace their diverse roles with grace and confidence, recognizing that they are capable of achieving excellence in every aspect of their lives.

Compassion And Wisdom

While Durga Maa is known for her ferocity in battle, she is also revered for her compassion and wisdom. This duality highlights the importance of nurturing qualities alongside strength. Modern women, in their quest for success and independence, can draw from Durga Maa's example to cultivate compassion, empathy, and wisdom. These qualities are essential not only for personal growth but also for building strong, supportive communities and fostering meaningful relationships.

Self-respect And Dignity

Durga Maa commands respect and reverence wherever she goes. Her stories often emphasize the importance of self-respect and dignity. In today's society, where women frequently encounter situations that challenge their self-worth, Durga Maa's teachings remind them to uphold their dignity and never settle for less than they deserve. This message is particularly crucial in promoting self-confidence and assertiveness among women, encouraging them to demand and receive the respect they are entitled to.

Spiritual Connection And Inner Peace

In the hustle and bustle of modern life, maintaining a connection with one's spiritual side can provide immense strength and peace. Durga Maa's stories and the rituals of Navratras offer a pathway to spiritual enlightenment and inner tranquility. For modern women, engaging with these traditions can be a source of solace and a means to recharge their spirits amidst daily stresses. It helps them reconnect with their inner selves and find balance in a fast-paced world.

Role Models And Mentors

The nine forms of Durga Maa, each with their unique attributes and stories, serve as diverse role models for women. From Shailaputri's steadfastness to Mahagauri's purity and compassion, each avatar offers lessons that are applicable to various aspects of life. Modern women can look up to these divine forms as mentors, drawing inspiration and guidance from their stories to navigate their own journeys.

In conclusion, the teachings and stories of Durga Maa are not relics of the past but dynamic, living principles that hold great relevance for the modern woman. They offer lessons in empowerment, resilience, balance, compassion, self-respect, and spiritual growth. By embracing these timeless narratives, modern women can find strength, inspiration, and a deeper connection to their cultural heritage, empowering them to lead lives of purpose and fulfillment

My Real Life Story: A Divine Blessing

For as long as I can remember, Durga Maa has been the pillar of my faith. Through life's trials and tribulations, her presence has always been a source of strength and comfort. In this chapter, I share a deeply personal story that not only tested my faith but also reaffirmed it in the most miraculous way.

The First Loss Two years before the birth of my younger son, I experienced an unimaginable loss. My second child, a beautiful baby boy, lived for only ten hours. The pain of losing him was indescribable, and the grief that followed seemed insurmountable. During this dark period, my faith in Durga Maa wavered, yet I clung to it, hoping for solace.

The Birth of My Younger Son When I became pregnant again, my heart was filled with both joy and anxiety. The day my younger son was born, I hoped for a new beginning. However, shortly after his birth, he struggled to breathe. The doctors worked desperately to revive him, and he was quickly placed in the ICU. Fear gripped me as memories of my first loss resurfaced.

The Power of Prayer In that moment of despair, I turned to Durga Maa, pleading for my son's life. Exhausted and overwhelmed, I prayed with all my heart. The doctors gave me an injection to help me sleep. As I slept, I had a dream that would change everything. I saw myself in a temple, weeping before Durga Maa's idol. Suddenly, Maa threw a rose flower towards me. I woke up with a sense of calm and immediately shared my dream with my grandmother.

The Grandmother's Interpretation My grandmother, a woman of deep faith, listened to my dream and smiled. She told me that Durga Maa had indeed blessed my son. The flower was a symbol of her blessing, and I should be at peace. Her words brought me immense comfort and hope.

Recovery and Renewal of Faith Miraculously, my son began to recover. Each passing day brought signs of improvement, and soon, he was strong enough to come home. This experience fortified my faith in Durga Maa and deepened my devotion. I felt a profound sense of gratitude for the divine intervention that saved my son's life.

Fulfilling the Promise In my prayers, I had promised Durga Maa that I would take my son to Vaishno Devi if he recovered. When he turned one year old, I fulfilled that promise. We traveled to Vaishno Devi, and there, we performed his mundan ceremony. It was a moment of immense joy and gratitude, a testament to the power of faith and the blessings of Durga Maa.

Reflection and Conclusion This experience has left an indelible mark on my heart and soul. It has taught me the true power of faith and the importance of hope, even in the darkest of times.

I share this story with you, dear reader, to inspire and remind you that the divine presence of Durga Maa is always with us, guiding and protecting us through life's challenges.

Significance of Durga Maa

Durga Maa, also known as Goddess Durga, holds immense significance in Hinduism. She is revered as a powerful deity who embodies the combined energies of all the gods and represents the divine feminine force. Here are the key aspects of her significance:

1. Symbol of Strength and Power

- **Warrior Goddess**: Durga is often depicted riding a lion or tiger, symbolizing her fearlessness and strength. She is portrayed with multiple arms, each carrying a weapon, signifying her power to combat evil and protect the righteous.

- **Victory Over Evil**: She is celebrated for her victory over the buffalo demon Mahishasura, symbolizing the triumph of good over evil.

2. Embodiment of Shakti

- **Divine Feminine Energy**: Durga represents Shakti, the divine feminine energy that is the source of all creation, preservation, and destruction in the universe.

- **Dynamic Force**: She embodies the dynamic and active aspect of the divine, as opposed to the passive and contemplative nature represented by other deities.

3. Protector and Preserver

- **Guardian of the Universe**: Durga is believed to protect the universe from evil forces and restore balance and harmony.

- **Motherly Figure**: As a mother goddess, she is compassionate and nurturing, offering protection and guidance to her devotees.

4. Representation of Various Virtues

- **Courage and Determination**: Durga inspires her devotees to be courageous and determined in the face of challenges.

- **Righteousness and Justice**: She upholds righteousness (dharma) and justice, teaching the importance of ethical and moral living.

5. Central Figure in Festivals

- **Navratri**: The festival of Navratri, which spans nine nights, is dedicated to the worship of Durga in her various forms. Each day honors a different aspect of the goddess, celebrating her diverse attributes and stories.

- **Durga Puja**: In West Bengal and other parts of India, Durga Puja is a major festival that involves elaborate rituals, processions, and cultural performances to honor the goddess.

6. Inspiration for Women

- **Empowerment**: Durga serves as a symbol of empowerment for women, embodying strength, independence, and resilience.

- **Role Model**: Her stories and attributes inspire women to embrace their inner power and assertiveness.

7. Spiritual Significance

- **Path to Liberation**: Worshiping Durga is believed to help devotees overcome their inner demons and impurities, leading them towards spiritual liberation (moksha).
- **Meditative Practices**: Chanting her mantras and meditating on her image are considered powerful spiritual practices that bring peace and enlightenment.

8. Cultural and Artistic Influence

- **Art and Literature**: Durga has inspired countless works of art, literature, music, and dance, reflecting her profound influence on Hindu culture.

- **Mythology and Folklore**: Her stories and legends are integral parts of Hindu mythology and folklore, enriching the cultural heritage of India.

9. Integration of Various Deities

- **Unity of Divine Forces**: Durga is believed to be a unified form of various goddesses like Parvati, Lakshmi, and Saraswati, each representing different aspects of the divine feminine. This integration symbolizes the unity of all divine forces in the universe.

10. Global Recognition

- **Beyond India**: While Durga is primarily worshiped in India, her influence extends globally, with Hindu communities around the world celebrating her festivals and honoring her significance.

Durga Maa's significance is multifaceted, encompassing spiritual, cultural, ethical, and social dimensions. She remains a central figure in Hinduism, inspiring devotion, reverence, and admiration from millions of followers.

Overview of Navratras

Navratras, also known as Navratri, is a major Hindu festival celebrated over nine nights and ten days, dedicated to the worship of the divine feminine in various forms. Here's an overview of Navratras:

1. Etymology and Meaning:

- **Navratri:** The term "Navratri" comes from the Sanskrit words "nava" (nine) and "ratri" (night), meaning "nine nights."

- **Purpose:** It is a festival that celebrates the victory of good over evil and honors the goddess Durga and her various forms.

2. Timing and Types:

- **Twice a Year:** Navratri is celebrated twice a year: Chaitra Navratri in the spring (March-April) and Sharad Navratri in the autumn (September-October).

- **Sharad Navratri:** The most widely celebrated and significant Navratri, leading up to Dussehra, which marks the victory of Lord Rama over Ravana and Durga over Mahishasura.

- **Chaitra Navratri:** Concludes with Ram Navami, the birthday of Lord Rama.

- **Other Navratris:** There are two lesser-known Navratris—Magha Navratri and Ashada Navratri—celebrated by specific communities.

3. Significance:

- **Devotion to the Goddess:** Each of the nine days is dedicated to a different form of Durga, representing various aspects of her power and virtues.

- **Spiritual Renewal:** A time for spiritual introspection, fasting, and purification.

- **Cultural Importance:** Involves various cultural activities, traditional music, dance, and rituals.

4. The Nine Days:

Each day of Navratri is dedicated to a specific form of Durga, and the rituals and prayers focus on the particular attributes of that form:

- **Day 1 - Shailaputri:** Worship of Shailaputri, the daughter of the mountains, symbolizing strength and purity.

- **Day 2 - Brahmacharini:** Devotion to Brahmacharini, representing penance and devotion.

- **Day 3 - Chandraghanta:** Honor Chandraghanta, the goddess of peace and serenity.

- **Day 4 - Kushmanda:** Worship Kushmanda, the creator of the universe.

- **Day 5 - Skandamata:** Devotion to Skandamata, the mother of Skanda (Kartikeya), symbolizing motherly love.

- **Day 6 - Katyayani:** Worship of Katyayani, a warrior goddess.

- **Day 7 - Kalaratri:** Honor Kalaratri, the fierce and destructive form of Durga.

- **Day 8 - Mahagauri:** Devotion to Mahagauri, symbolizing purity and calm.

- **Day 9 - Siddhidatri:** Worship Siddhidatri, the giver of supernatural powers.

5. Rituals and Practices:

- **Fasting:** Many devotees observe fasting, consuming only specific foods or abstaining from certain foods.

- **Puja and Aarti:** Daily rituals include special pujas, aartis, and recitations of sacred texts.

- **Garba and Dandiya:** In Gujarat and some other regions, traditional dance forms like Garba and Dandiya are performed.

6. Regional Variations:

- **Durga Puja:** In West Bengal, Assam, and other eastern states, Durga Puja is a major celebration that coincides with the last five days of Navratri.

- **Golu:** In Tamil Nadu, Karnataka, and Andhra Pradesh, Golu (or Kolu) involves the display of dolls and figurines on tiered steps.

- **Bathukamma:** In Telangana, Bathukamma, a floral festival, is celebrated.

7. Climax and Dussehra:

- **Ninth Day (Navami):** Culminates with Kanya Puja, where young girls are worshiped as representations of the divine feminine.

- **Dussehra:** The tenth day, also known as Vijayadashami, marks the victory of good over evil, symbolized by the defeat of Ravana by Lord Rama and Mahishasura by Goddess Durga.

8. Spiritual and Cultural Impact:

- **Unity and Community:** Brings together communities, fostering a sense of unity and shared cultural heritage.

- **Renewal and Reflection:** Encourages personal reflection, renewal, and adherence to ethical and spiritual values.

Navratri is a vibrant and multifaceted festival that holds deep spiritual, cultural, and social significance, celebrated with devotion, enthusiasm, and joy across India and among Hindu communities worldwide.

CHAPTER TWO

The Mythology and Legends of Durga Maa

The origins of Durga Maa in Hindu mythology are rich and complex, with her story deeply embedded in the cosmic struggle between good and evil. Here is a detailed discussion of her origins and background:

1. The Concept of Shakti

- **Divine Feminine Power**: Durga is a principal form of the Goddess, also known as Devi or Shakti in Hinduism. Shakti is the cosmic energy that represents the feminine principle and is responsible for creation, preservation, and destruction.

- **Embodiment of Energy**: Durga embodies this dynamic energy, symbolizing the power of the gods and the universal force that maintains the cosmic order.

2. Creation of Durga

- **The Birth of Durga**: According to Hindu mythology, Durga was created by the collective energies of the gods. This event took place to combat the demon Mahishasura, who had become invincible due to a boon that he could not be killed by any man or god.

- **Combined Powers**: The gods, realizing that they could not defeat Mahishasura on their own, combined their powers to create a supreme goddess. Durga emerged, radiant and powerful, endowed with the strengths and weapons of various gods.

3. Attributes and Iconography

- **Symbolic Weapons**: Each god contributed a weapon to Durga. For example, Shiva gave her a trident, Vishnu a discus, and Indra a thunderbolt. These weapons symbolize her role as a warrior goddess.

- **Iconography**: Durga is typically depicted riding a lion or tiger, which represents her mastery over power, will, and determination. She is shown with multiple arms, each holding a weapon or item that signifies her divine attributes.

4. The Legend of Mahishasura

- **Demon King**: Mahishasura, a buffalo demon, performed severe penance and obtained a boon from Brahma that no man or god could kill him, making him arrogant and tyrannical.

- **Divine Battle**: Durga waged a fierce battle against Mahishasura and his army for nine days and nights. On the tenth day, known as Vijayadashami or Dussehra, she finally defeated and killed Mahishasura, restoring peace and order to the world.

5. Vedic and Puranic References

- **Vedic Mentions**: While direct references to Durga are not prominent in the earliest Vedic texts, the concept of a powerful, protective goddess can be traced back to the Vedic hymns that praise divine feminine energy.

- **Puranic Narratives**: The detailed stories of Durga's creation and her battles are found in various Puranas, particularly the Markandeya Purana, which includes the Devi Mahatmya (also known as the Durga Saptashati or Chandi Path).

6. Symbolism and Interpretations

- **Triumph of Good Over Evil**: Durga's battle with Mahishasura symbolizes the eternal struggle between good and evil. Her victory represents the triumph of righteousness and the destruction of malevolent forces.

- **Universal Mother**: Durga is also seen as the universal mother, nurturing and protecting her devotees. She embodies compassion, strength, and benevolence, guiding her followers towards a virtuous life.

7. Cultural and Religious Significance

- **Worship and Festivals**: Durga is widely worshipped across India and beyond, with major festivals like Navratri and Durga Puja dedicated to her. These festivals celebrate her victory over Mahishasura and honor her various forms.

- **Regional Variations**: Different regions have their own unique ways of venerating Durga, reflecting local traditions and cultural practices. In Bengal, for example, Durga Puja is a grand celebration marked by elaborate rituals, processions, and artistic displays.

8. Philosophical Aspects

- **Adi Parashakti**: In the Shakta tradition, Durga is often identified with Adi Parashakti, the supreme goddess who is the source of all other goddesses and the ultimate reality.

- **Maya and Liberation**: Durga's association with Maya (the illusory nature of the material world) and her role in guiding souls towards liberation (moksha) are key philosophical themes in Hindu thought.

The origins of Durga Maa are thus a blend of mythological narratives, symbolic representations, and philosophical concepts that highlight her central role in Hinduism as a powerful, protective, and nurturing deity.

The Story of Mahishasura

The story of Mahishasura is a central narrative in Hindu mythology, particularly in the context of the goddess Durga's divine mission. Here is a detailed account of the legend:

1. Background and Boon of Mahishasura:

- **Asura King**: Mahishasura was a powerful demon (asura) with the ability to change his form at will. He often took the shape of a buffalo, hence his name "Mahisha" which means buffalo in Sanskrit.

- **Severe Penance**: Seeking invincibility, Mahishasura performed intense penance to please Lord Brahma, the creator god.

- **Boon Granted**: Impressed by his austerities, Brahma granted Mahishasura a boon that no man or god could kill him. Overconfident, Mahishasura believed he was invincible as he did not consider the possibility of a woman defeating him.

2. Rise to Power:

- **Conquest and Tyranny**: Empowered by the boon, Mahishasura embarked on a campaign of conquest, defeating gods and taking over the heavens (Swarga). He drove the gods out and established himself as the ruler of the universe.

- **Chaos and Fear**: His reign brought chaos, fear, and suffering to the cosmos. The gods, unable to defeat him, were left helpless and sought a solution to end his tyranny.

3. Creation of Durga:

- **Appeal to the Trinity**: The gods, led by Brahma, Vishnu, and Shiva, approached the Trinity (Trimurti) and requested help. The combined anger and energy of the gods created a radiant beam of light, from which emerged Durga, the supreme goddess.

- **Divine Weapons**: Each god endowed Durga with their own special weapons. Shiva gave her a trident (trishula), Vishnu a discus (chakra), Indra a thunderbolt (vajra), and so on. She also received a lion as her mount, symbolizing strength and fearlessness.

4. The Battle:

- **Confrontation**: Durga, radiating divine power and equipped with celestial weapons, rode her lion to confront Mahishasura. The battlefield witnessed a fierce and epic battle between the goddess and the demon army.

- **Shape-Shifting**: Mahishasura, using his boon, transformed into various forms, including a buffalo, an elephant, and a lion, to confuse and overpower Durga. However, she skillfully countered each form with her agility and divine prowess.

- **Final Duel**: The battle raged for nine days and nights. On the tenth day, Durga managed to overpower Mahishasura. As he transformed back into a buffalo, she pounced on him, pinning him down with her foot and piercing his heart with her trident, finally killing him.

5. Symbolism and Significance:

- **Triumph of Good Over Evil**: The victory of Durga over Mahishasura symbolizes the triumph of good over evil and the restoration of cosmic order.

- **Divine Feminine Power**: The story emphasizes the power and significance of the divine feminine. Despite the boon protecting Mahishasura from men and gods, he was defeated by a woman, highlighting the strength and capabilities of women.

- **Moral Lessons**: The tale serves as a reminder that arrogance and misuse of power lead to downfall, and that righteousness and justice will ultimately prevail.

6. Cultural and Religious Impact:

- **Durga Puja**: The story is celebrated with great fervor during Durga Puja in Bengal and other parts of India. Elaborate idols of Durga slaying Mahishasura are created, and the victory is commemorated with rituals, feasting, and cultural events.

- **Navratri**: The nine-day festival of Navratri, observed in many parts of India, celebrates the nine forms of Durga and culminates with Vijayadashami (Dussehra), marking her victory over Mahishasura.

7. Retellings and Variations:

- **Mythological Texts**: The story of Mahishasura is recounted in various Hindu scriptures, including the Devi Mahatmya (part of the Markandeya Purana), the Skanda Purana, and the Devi Bhagavata Purana.

- **Regional Variations**: Different regions of India have their own versions and retellings of the story, each adding unique elements and interpretations while maintaining the core message.

• 16 •

The legend of Mahishasura and his defeat by Durga Maa is a powerful and enduring myth that highlights the virtues of courage, righteousness, and the divine power of the feminine. It continues to inspire and be celebrated by millions of devotees around the world.

Interesting Stories and Legends Associated with Durga Maa

Durga Maa is a central figure in Hindu mythology, and numerous legends and stories highlight her divine power, courage, and protective nature. Here are some key stories and legends associated with Durga Maa:

1. Slaying of Mahishasura

- *The Legend:* One of the most famous legends associated with Durga Maa is her battle with the buffalo demon Mahishasura. As detailed earlier, Mahishasura was a powerful demon who, due to a boon from Brahma, could not be killed by any man or god. In response to the havoc he caused, the gods created Durga from their collective energies and armed her with their most potent weapons. Durga fought Mahishasura and his army for nine days and nights, ultimately slaying him on the tenth day, symbolizing the triumph of good over evil.

2. Shumbha and Nishumbha

- *The Legend*: During a fierce battle against two powerful demons, Shumbha and Nishumbha, Durga created another powerful goddess from her forehead to aid her. This goddess was Kali, who emerged with intense anger and unparalleled ferocity. Kali, with her terrifying appearance and insatiable hunger for destruction, annihilated the demon armies and ultimately killed Shumbha and Nishumbha. Kali's birth story highlights Durga's ability to manifest different aspects of herself to conquer evil.

3. The Slaying of Dhumralochana

- *The Legend:* Dhumralochana, a demon general of Shumbha and Nishumbha, was sent to capture Durga. When he confronted her, Durga's lion roared fiercely, stunning Dhumralochana. Durga then effortlessly turned him to ashes with a single hum. This legend demonstrates Durga's effortless power and her divine protection over the world.

4. The Destruction of Raktabija

- *The Legend:* Raktabija was another formidable demon with a unique boon: every drop of his blood that touched the ground would create a clone of himself. During the battle, whenever Durga attacked him and his blood spilled, countless Raktabijas were born. To counter this, Durga called upon Kali, who spread her tongue over the battlefield to catch every drop of blood before it could touch the ground. Kali then devoured Raktabija and all his clones, ensuring they could not regenerate. This story illustrates Durga's strategic brilliance and her ability to overcome seemingly insurmountable challenges.

5. The Marriage of Shiva and Parvati

- *The Legend:* Durga is also known as Parvati, the consort of Lord Shiva. According to legend, Parvati, an incarnation of Sati, performed severe penance to win Shiva's heart after Sati's self-immolation. Despite Shiva's initial indifference due to his deep meditation and grief over Sati's death, Parvati's devotion and determination eventually led Shiva to accept her as his wife. Their union symbolizes the balance of cosmic energies and the harmony between male and female principles.

6. Durga as Mahishasuramardini

- *The Legend:* In this form, Durga is worshipped as the great warrior goddess who rides a lion and battles the forces of evil. Mahishasuramardini, meaning "the slayer of Mahishasura," is a title that emphasizes her role as the protector of the universe. Temples and statues often depict her in this victorious pose, highlighting her strength and courage.

7. The Killing of Madhu and Kaitabha

- *The Legend:* According to the Devi Bhagavata Purana, Madhu and Kaitabha were two demons born from the earwax of Lord Vishnu while he was in deep sleep. They planned to kill Brahma, who sought Vishnu's help. Vishnu, however, was in a deep slumber under the influence of Yoga Nidra, personified by the goddess Mahamaya (another form of Durga). Brahma prayed to Mahamaya to awaken Vishnu. Once awake, Vishnu fought the demons for thousands of years but couldn't defeat them due to a boon they had received. At Vishnu's request, Mahamaya withdrew her influence, and Vishnu was able to kill the demons. This story highlights Durga's role as the cosmic power behind the gods.

8. The Tale of Durga and the Buffalo Demon (Markandeya Purana)

- *The Legend:* In the Devi Mahatmya section of the Markandeya Purana, Durga is described in her battle against the buffalo demon Mahishasura. This scripture vividly describes the creation of Durga from the combined energies of all the gods, her formidable appearance, and her ultimate victory over Mahishasura. The Devi Mahatmya is recited and revered during the Navratri festival, emphasizing Durga's role as the supreme goddess who restores cosmic balance.

9. Durga and the Demon Durgamasura

- *The Legend:* Another legend speaks of the demon Durgamasura, who performed severe penance and received a boon that made him very powerful. He misused his power to torment the gods and humans. The gods prayed to the divine mother for help, and Durga appeared to defeat Durgamasura. Her name, Durga, meaning "the invincible," is believed to have originated from this legend.

These legends and stories reflect Durga Maa's multifaceted nature as a warrior, protector, mother, and embodiment of divine energy. They serve to inspire and instill devotion among her followers, illustrating her timeless relevance and power.

The Story of Rama and Ravana Leading to Navratri

During the epic battle between Rama and Ravana, there came a day when Rama sat looking despondent. Noticing his sorrow, Sugriva approached him and asked why he was so sad. Rama replied, "I am fighting this war for a just cause, to rescue my wife Sita. Yet, Ravana, who is on the path of adharma (unrighteousness), seems to be winning. Today was a particularly bad day for me. I saw that Durga Maa was behind Ravana. Why is she supporting him and not me?"

Sugriva explained, "Ravana has performed intense penance and devotion to Durga Maa, which is why she is aiding him in battle. To gain her favor, you too must worship her with equal devotion."

Taking Sugriva's advice to heart, Rama began a rigorous worship of Durga Maa for nine consecutive days. Each day, he offered her a beautiful lotus flower. On the ninth day, Durga Maa decided to test Rama's devotion. She hid the ninth lotus flower, knowing Rama would not be able to complete his penance without it.

When Rama discovered the missing flower, he was distraught. He remembered his mother's words from his childhood, telling him that his eyes were as beautiful as lotus flowers. Resolute in his devotion, Rama decided to offer one of his eyes in place of the missing lotus flower. As he was about to remove his eye, Durga Maa appeared before him, moved by his unwavering devotion and willingness to sacrifice.

Durga Maa blessed Rama, assuring him of his victory over Ravana. With her blessings, Rama's fortunes in battle changed. He defeated Ravana and rescued Sita. Rama's triumphant return to Ayodhya is celebrated as Diwali, marking the victory of good over evil and the return of light.

The nine days of Rama's worship of Durga Maa are commemorated as Navratri, a period of nine nights dedicated to the nine forms of the goddess. The festival culminates in Dussehra, symbolizing Rama's victory over Ravana. This story highlights the power of devotion and the triumph of righteousness, serving as the foundation for these significant Hindu festivals.

The Iconography and Attributes of Durga Maa

The iconography and attributes of Durga Maa are rich with symbolism, reflecting her multifaceted nature and the various aspects of divine power and protection she embodies. Here is an explanation of the key symbols and attributes associated with Durga Maa:

1. Multiple Arms

- **Symbolism**: Durga is often depicted with multiple arms, usually eight or ten, each holding a different weapon or item. The multiple arms signify her omnipotence and ability to perform multiple tasks simultaneously.

- **Representation**: This symbolizes her divine powers to protect her devotees from all directions and destroy evil from all sides.

2. Weapons

Each weapon in Durga's hands has a specific symbolic meaning and represents the collective power of the gods who bestowed these upon her:

- **Trident (Trishula)**: Given by Shiva, it symbolizes the destruction of evil and ignorance.

- **Discus (Sudharshana Chakra)**: Given by Vishnu, it represents the cyclical nature of time and the universe and the power to destroy evil.

- **Conch Shell (Shankha)**: Given by Varuna, it symbolizes the primordial sound of creation (Om) and the call to divine action.

- **Bow and Arrow**: Given by Vayu (the wind god), these represent energy, potential, and the focus needed to overcome adversities.

- **Thunderbolt (Vajra)**: Given by Indra, it symbolizes firmness of spirit and the power to eliminate obstacles.

- **Sword (Khadga)**: Represents knowledge, sharpness of intellect, and the destruction of ignorance and falsehood.

- **Club (Gada)**: Given by Hanuman, it represents strength, authority, and the ability to uproot evil.

- **Lotus (Padma)**: Symbolizes purity, self-realization, and spiritual awakening. The lotus remains pure despite growing in muddy water, representing spiritual transcendence.

3. Lion or Tiger Mount (Vahana)

- **Symbolism**: Durga is often shown riding a lion or tiger. The lion symbolizes power, will, and determination. Riding the lion signifies Durga's mastery over these qualities and her role as a protector of righteousness (dharma).

- **Representation**: This also indicates her fearless and courageous nature in confronting evil.

4. Divine Attire and Ornaments

- **Red Saree**: Durga is often depicted wearing a red saree, which symbolizes action, power, and the ferocity of her energy. Red is also the color of fertility and blood, representing life force and the cycles of creation.

- **Crown**: The crown she wears signifies her supreme sovereignty over the universe.

- **Jewelry**: Her jewelry represents prosperity, abundance, and the richness of the divine.

5. The Lotus Seat

- **Symbolism**: Durga is sometimes depicted seated on a lotus, symbolizing divine origin and purity. The lotus signifies spiritual enlightenment and detachment from the material world despite being in it.

6. Three Eyes

- **Symbolism**: Durga is often portrayed with three eyes. Her left eye represents desire (the moon), the right eye represents action (the sun), and the central eye on her forehead represents knowledge (fire). This signifies her ability to see beyond the ordinary and her omniscient nature.

7. Serene Expression

- **Symbolism**: Despite being in the midst of battle, Durga's face is often shown with a serene and composed expression. This represents her inner peace, divine tranquility, and the assurance she provides to her devotees.

8. The Demon Mahishasura

- **Symbolism**: In many depictions, Durga is shown in the act of slaying the buffalo demon Mahishasura. This symbolizes the victory of good over evil and the protection of the righteous.

- **Representation**: It represents the subjugation of ego, ignorance, and demonic tendencies.

9. The Auspicious Aura

- **Symbolism**: Durga is often surrounded by a radiant aura, symbolizing her divine and celestial nature. This aura represents her spiritual energy that purifies and sanctifies her surroundings.

10. Mudras (Hand Gestures)

- **Abhaya Mudra**: One hand is often depicted in the Abhaya Mudra (gesture of fearlessness), symbolizing protection, reassurance, and blessing.

- **Varada Mudra**: Another hand might be in the Varada Mudra (gesture of granting boons), representing generosity and compassion.

11. Associated Animals

- **Lion/Tiger**: Symbolizes the control of power and energy.

- **Buffalo**: Represents ignorance and the demonic qualities that Durga vanquishes.

12. Surrounding Deities and Attendants

- **Symbolism**: In some depictions, Durga is accompanied by her children – Ganesha, Kartikeya, Lakshmi, and Saraswati. This symbolizes her role as the universal mother and nurturer of all creation.

The iconography of Durga Maa is a powerful visual language that conveys her divine attributes, her role as a protector and mother, and the deep philosophical concepts of Hinduism. Each element in her depiction is laden with meaning, reinforcing her status as a supreme and multifaceted deity.

CHAPTER FIVE

The Significance of Navratras

Navratras, also known as Navratri, hold immense religious, cultural, & spiritual significance in Hinduism. The festival, celebrated twice a year, is dedicated to the worship of the divine feminine & spans nine nights & ten days. Here is a detailed look at the significance of Navratras:

1. Religious Significance:

- **Divine Feminine Energy**: Navratras are dedicated to the worship of Durga Maa, the divine feminine energy (Shakti) in her various forms. Each day of Navratri is devoted to one of her nine avatars, symbolizing different aspects of her power & virtues.

- **Victory of Good Over Evil**: The festival commemorates the victory of Durga over the buffalo demon Mahishasura, symbolizing the triumph of good over evil. This narrative reinforces the idea that righteousness & virtue will ultimately prevail.

2. Spiritual Significance:

- **Self-Purification & Renewal**: Navratri is a time for self-purification, introspection, & spiritual renewal. Devotees observe fasting, engage in prayers, & practice meditation to cleanse their mind, body, & soul.

- **Inner Transformation**: The nine days symbolize the journey from ignorance to wisdom, from darkness to light, & from suffering to liberation. Devotees seek to embody the virtues of Durga & transform their lives through devotion & discipline.

3. Cultural Significance:

- **Community & Unity**: Navratri brings people together in celebration, fostering a sense of community & unity. It is marked by social gatherings, cultural performances, & collective rituals.

- **Cultural Heritage**: The festival showcases the rich cultural heritage of India through traditional music, dance, art, & rituals. It serves as a platform for preserving & promoting cultural traditions.

4. Seasonal & Agricultural Significance:

- **Harvest Festival**: Navratri coincides with important agricultural cycles. Sharad Navratri, celebrated in the autumn, marks the end of the monsoon season & the beginning of the harvest. It is a time to thank the divine for a bountiful harvest & seek blessings for future prosperity.

- **Seasonal Transition**: Chaitra Navratri, celebrated in the spring, marks the onset of the new season. It is a time to celebrate the renewal of life & the blossoming of nature.

5. The Nine Days & Their Significance:

Each day of Navratri is dedicated to a different form of Durga, with specific rituals & prayers that highlight her various aspects:

- **Day 1 - Shailaputri:**
  Significance: Worship of Shailaputri, the daughter of the mountains, symbolizes purity & strength.

  Rituals: Devotees invoke her blessings for strength & resolve.

- **Day 2 - Brahmacharini:**
  Significance: Devotion to Brahmacharini, the goddess of penance & austerity, represents spiritual knowledge & discipline.

Rituals: Devotees seek her blessings for perseverance & commitment to spiritual practices.

- **Day 3 - Ch&raghanta**:
  Significance: Honor Ch&raghanta, the goddess of peace & serenity, who represents courage & valor.

  Rituals: Devotees pray for bravery & protection against evil.

- **Day 4 - Kushm&a**:
  Significance: Worship Kushm&a, the creator of the universe, symbolizes the power of creation & abundance.

  Rituals: Devotees seek her blessings for health, wealth, & prosperity.

- **Day 5 - Sk&amata**:
  Significance: Devotion to Sk&amata, the mother of Sk&a (Kartikeya), represents maternal love & nurturing.

  Rituals: Devotees pray for the well-being & happiness of their families.

- **Day 6 - Katyayani**:
  Significance: Worship Katyayani, a fierce warrior goddess, symbolizes the destruction of evil & the protection of righteousness.

  Rituals: Devotees seek her blessings for strength to overcome challenges.

- **Day 7 - Kalaratri**:
  Significance: Honor Kalaratri, the dark & fearsome form of Durga, represents the destruction of ignorance & darkness.

Rituals: Devotees pray for protection & the removal of negativity from their lives.

- **Day 8 - Mahagauri**:
  Significance: Devotion to Mahagauri, the goddess of purity & calmness, symbolizes wisdom & inner peace.

  Rituals: Devotees seek her blessings for clarity of mind & spiritual growth.

- **Day 9 - Siddhidatri**:
  Significance: Worship Siddhidatri, the giver of supernatural powers & knowledge, represents the fulfillment of desires & spiritual aspirations.

  Rituals: Devotees pray for the attainment of spiritual & worldly goals.

6. Climax & Culmination:

- **Ninth Day (Navami)**: The ninth day of Navratri is often marked by Kanya Puja, where young girls are worshiped as manifestations of the divine feminine. This ritual signifies the nurturing & protective aspect of the goddess.

- **Vijayadashami (Dussehra)**: The festival culminates on the tenth day, known as Vijayadashami or Dussehra, which celebrates the victory of Durga over Mahishasura & the victory of Lord Rama over Ravana. It is a day of celebration, marking the triumph of good over evil.

7. Regional Variations:

- **Durga Puja**: In West Bengal, Assam, & other eastern states, Durga Puja is celebrated with gr&eur, particularly focusing on the last five days of Navratri. It involves elaborate rituals, idol processions, cultural performances, & community feasts.

- **Golu**: In Tamil Nadu, Karnataka, & &hra Pradesh, Golu (or Kolu) involves the display of dolls & figurines on tiered steps, representing various scenes from mythology & daily life. It is a time for social visits & cultural exchange.

- **Bathukamma**: In Telangana, Bathukamma, a floral festival, is celebrated with women arranging flowers in a conical shape & singing traditional songs.

8. Personal & Social Significance:

- **Devotion & Discipline**: Navratri encourages personal discipline through fasting, prayer, & meditation. It fosters a sense of devotion & reverence towards the divine.

- **Community Bonding**: The festival strengthens social bonds as families & communities come together to celebrate, share meals, & participate in cultural activities.

9. Economic Impact:

- **Festive Economy**: Navratri has a significant economic impact, with increased sales in textiles, jewelry, sweets, & other festive goods. It also boosts tourism in regions known for gr& celebrations.

- **Art & Craft:** The festival supports local artisans & craftsmen who create idols, decorations, & traditional attire, preserving & promoting indigenous arts & crafts.

- **Navratri is a festival that encompasses** religious devotion, spiritual growth, cultural richness, social unity, & economic vitality. It is a time to honor the divine feminine, celebrate the triumph of good over evil, & rejuvenate oneself through practices of faith & community engagement.

Historical Context

The celebration of Navratras (or Navratri) has a rich historical and cultural background that spans centuries. Understanding this context involves exploring its origins, evolution, and significance throughout Indian history. Here's a detailed overview of the historical context of Navratras:

1. Ancient Origins:
Vedic Period (1500–500 BCE):

- **Early References:** The roots of Navratri can be traced back to the Vedic period, where the worship of deities was central to spiritual practices. While there is no direct mention of Navratri in Vedic texts, the period laid the foundation for future religious rituals and festivals.

- **Concept of Shakti:** The Vedic hymns and rituals often invoked feminine deities and energies, hinting at the early reverence for Shakti (divine feminine energy), which later became a focal point of Navratri celebrations.

Epic and Puranic Literature (500 BCE–500 CE):

- **Devi Mahatmya:** One of the earliest and most important texts for the worship of the goddess is the Devi Mahatmya (also known as Durga Saptashati or Chandi Path), part of the Markandeya Purana. It narrates the story of Durga's battle with Mahishasura and forms the scriptural basis for many of the rituals performed during Navratri.

- **Puranic Stories:** The Puranas, ancient Hindu texts that include mythological stories, describe the origins of the goddess Durga and the significance of her forms. The stories of Durga's victories over demons like Mahishasura were elaborated in these texts, providing a mythological framework for Navratri.

2. Historical Evolution:
Medieval Period (500–1500 CE):

- **Regional Practices:** During the medieval period, the celebration of Navratri became more elaborate and regionally varied. Temples dedicated to Durga and other forms of the goddess began to be established across India.

- **Integration of Local Traditions**: Local traditions and deities were integrated into the Navratri celebrations, leading to the diverse forms of the festival observed today. For instance, the Bengali Durga Puja evolved as a major celebration during this period.

- **Royal Patronage**: Many kings and rulers were patrons of the festival, organizing grand celebrations in their courts and cities. This period saw the flourishing of art, music, and dance associated with Navratri.

Renaissance Period (1500–1800 CE):

- **Art and Literature**: The Navratri festival inspired numerous works of art, literature, and music. This era saw the creation of elaborate temple decorations, classical dance forms, and devotional literature centered around Durga.

- **Bhakti Movement**: The Bhakti movement emphasized personal devotion to deities. Saints and poets from this movement celebrated Durga in their hymns and songs, further popularizing the festival.

Modern Era (1800–Present):
Colonial Period (1800–1947 CE):

- **Public Celebrations**: The 19th century saw the public celebration of festivals, including Navratri, become more organized. The influence of colonial rulers and the growth of nationalist movements led to a revival of traditional practices and the establishment of public Durga Puja celebrations.

- **Bengal Renaissance**: In Bengal, the 19th century Bengal Renaissance played a crucial role in the cultural and religious revival of Durga Puja. Prominent figures like Raja Ram Mohan Roy and later leaders like Surendranath Banerjee and the Tagore family were instrumental in shaping modern Durga Puja celebrations.

Post-Independence Era (1947–Present):

- **Nationwide Celebrations:** After India's independence in 1947, Navratri became a nationwide celebration, with diverse regional practices and a focus on both traditional and modern elements of the festival.

- **Globalization:** In recent decades, the celebration of Navratri has spread globally due to the Indian diaspora. Festivals are now celebrated in many countries outside India, showcasing the cultural richness of Navratri to a broader audience.

3. Cultural and Regional Variations:
North India:

- **Durga Puja:** In states like West Bengal, Bihar, and Assam, Navratri culminates in the grand celebration of Durga Puja, which includes elaborate pandals (temporary structures), artistic idols, and cultural performances.

South India:

- **Golu/Kolu:** In Tamil Nadu, Karnataka, and Andhra Pradesh, the festival includes the arrangement of dolls (Golu) depicting scenes from mythology and daily life, and visiting homes to view the displays.

West India:

- **Garba and Dandiya**: In Gujarat and parts of Maharashtra, Navratri is marked by the vibrant dance forms of Garba and Dandiya, accompanied by folk songs and traditional rituals.

East India:

- **Vijayadashami**: In Odisha, the festival culminates in the celebration of Vijayadashami, with the immersion of Durga idols and traditional processions.

4. Historical Texts and Scriptures:
Devi Bhagavata Purana:

- **Significance**: This Purana provides detailed accounts of the goddess's manifestations and the rituals associated with her worship, reinforcing the religious importance of Navratri.

Skanda Purana:

- **Significance**: This text also contains stories and hymns dedicated to Durga and her various forms, contributing to the historical understanding of Navratri practices.

5. Modern Celebrations:
Media and Technology:

- **Digital Platforms**: In the 21st century, Navratri celebrations have been amplified through social media, digital media, and television broadcasts, making the festival accessible to a global audience.

- **Innovation**: Modern celebrations include innovative approaches to traditional practices, such as virtual darshans (viewing of deities), online cultural events, and digital engagement with the festival's religious aspects.

Celebration of Navratras all over India

Navratras, or Navratri, are celebrated with diverse customs and traditions across India, reflecting the country's rich cultural tapestry. Each region adds its unique flavor to the festival, making it a vibrant and multifaceted celebration. Here's a detailed look at how Navratras are celebrated across different regions in India:

1. North India

Uttar Pradesh

- **Celebrations:** In Uttar Pradesh, especially in cities like Varanasi and Lucknow, Navratri is celebrated with devotional fervor. Temples are adorned with flowers and lights, and special prayers (pujas) are held each day. Devotees fast and participate in religious processions.

- **Rituals:** Traditional rituals include recitations of the Devi Mahatmya and Durga Saptashati. Kanya Puja is performed on the eighth or ninth day, where young girls are honored as manifestations of the goddess.

Himachal Pradesh

- **Celebrations:** The state celebrates Navratri with both religious and cultural activities. In towns like Mandi, the Mandi Mahotsav coincides with Navratri, featuring cultural performances, fairs, and processions.

- **Rituals:** Devotees participate in temple rituals, community feasts, and folk dances.

Punjab

- **Celebrations:** Navratri in Punjab is marked by vibrant Dandiya and Garba dances in communities. The festivities also include Chole Bhature and other traditional foods.

- **Rituals:** Temples hold special prayers, and there are processions featuring the idol of Durga. The festival also includes performances of traditional Punjabi folk songs and dances.

2. South India

Tamil Nadu

- **Celebrations**: In Tamil Nadu, Navratri is celebrated with the Golu (Kolu) festival. Homes are decorated with Bommai Golu displays featuring dolls and figurines arranged in tiers.

- **Rituals:** The Kolu displays depict scenes from mythology, everyday life, and significant events. Families invite friends and neighbors to view the Golu, perform prayers, and offer traditional sweets.

Karnataka

- **Celebrations**: Navratri in Karnataka is celebrated with a focus on the Golu tradition, where dolls representing various deities and mythological scenes are arranged in homes.

- **Rituals:** Temples conduct special pujas, and families engage in community gatherings, cultural performances, and traditional food preparation.

Andhra Pradesh

- **Celebrations:** In Andhra Pradesh, Navratri is celebrated with elaborate Koluvu displays, similar to Golu. The festival includes Sankranti celebrations and traditional dance forms.

- **Rituals:** Devotees perform special pujas, sing devotional songs, and prepare festive dishes. The Kolu displays feature deities and significant mythological scenes.

3. West India

Gujarat

- **Celebrations**: Gujarat is known for its grand Garba and Dandiya dance events during Navratri. The state hosts numerous Garba nights where people gather for dance and devotional singing.

- **Rituals:** Devotees observe fasts, perform pujas, and participate in Garba and Dandiya dances. There are also processions and fairs celebrating the goddess Durga.

Maharashtra

- **Celebrations**: In Maharashtra, Navratri includes both religious and cultural activities. The state is known for its vibrant Dandiya Raas and Garba events.

- **Rituals:** Temples and homes are decorated with flowers, and special prayers are offered. The festival also includes community celebrations and cultural performances.

4. East India

West Bengal

- **Celebrations**: West Bengal is famous for its elaborate Durga Puja celebrations during Navratri. The festival is marked by grand pandals (temporary structures) that house intricate Durga idols.

- **Rituals:** The last five days of Navratri, from Saptami to Dashami, are celebrated with large-scale processions, artistic decorations, cultural performances, and community feasts. The immersion of Durga idols on the final day marks the culmination of the festival.

Odisha

- **Celebrations:** In Odisha, Navratri culminates in the celebration of Vijayadashami, with the Durga Puja festival being a major event.

- **Rituals:** Temples hold elaborate rituals, and there are grand processions featuring the Durga idols. The festival is marked by cultural performances, including traditional dances and music.

5. Central India

Madhya Pradesh

- **Celebrations**: In Madhya Pradesh, Navratri is celebrated with devotion and cultural activities. Temples conduct special pujas, and there are community gatherings and fairs.

- **Rituals:** The festival includes fasting, prayer ceremonies, and traditional performances.

Chhattisgarh

- **Celebrations:** Navratri in Chhattisgarh is celebrated with a focus on the worship of Durga and other deities.

- **Rituals:** Devotees participate in temple rituals, community feasts, and cultural events.

6. Regional Highlights and Unique Practices

Kashmir

- **Celebrations:** In Kashmir, Navratri is observed with a mix of religious observances and cultural events.

- **Rituals:** Devotees engage in temple visits, prayer sessions, and community gatherings.

Assam

- **Celebrations**: Assam celebrates Navratri with the grand Durga Puja festivities.

- **Rituals:** Temples are adorned with elaborate decorations, and there are processions and community events centered around the worship of Durga.

CHAPTER SEVEN

Spiritual Practices During Navratri

The spiritual significance of Navratri (Navratras) is profound and multifaceted, extending beyond mere celebration to deep-rooted religious, philosophical, and transformative practices. Here's a detailed exploration of the spiritual importance of Navratri:

1. Embodiment of the Divine Feminine
   Divine Feminine Energy (Shakti)

- **Concept of Shakti**: At the heart of Navratri is the veneration of **Shakti**, the divine feminine energy that represents the creative force of the universe. Shakti is the source of all life and the divine power behind creation, preservation, and destruction.

- **Forms of Durga**: During Navratri, the worship of Durga in her various forms—Shailaputri, Brahmacharini, Chandraghanta, Kushmanda, Skandamata, Katyayani, Kalaratri, Mahagauri, and Siddhidatri—represents different aspects of Shakti, embodying virtues like courage, wisdom, purity, and grace.

2. Victory of Good Over Evil
Mythological Background

- **Mahishasura's Defeat**: One of the central spiritual narratives of Navratri is the story of **Durga's victory over Mahishasura**, the buffalo demon who symbolizes ignorance and evil. This victory signifies the triumph of righteousness over malevolence.

- **Symbolic Battle**: The battle between Durga and Mahishasura represents the inner struggle between good and evil, illustrating that spiritual strength and divine intervention can overcome the darkness of ignorance and negativity.

3. Path to Spiritual Transformation
Inner Journey and Self-Realization

- **Introspection and Reflection**: Navratri serves as a period for deep introspection, self-examination, and spiritual growth. Devotees use this time to reflect on their own lives, seeking to purify their hearts and minds.

- **Spiritual Practices**: The festival encourages practices such as **fasting, prayer, meditation,** and **chanting** of sacred hymns. These practices help devotees focus on their spiritual goals and foster a deeper connection with the divine.

4. Cultivation of Virtues and Discipline
Fasting and Rituals

- **Spiritual Discipline**: Observing fasts and engaging in daily rituals during Navratri are forms of spiritual discipline that help devotees practice self-control and devotion.

- **Ethical Conduct**: The festival emphasizes ethical living and personal discipline, encouraging devotees to abstain from negative behaviors and focus on virtues such as compassion, humility, and respect.

5. Celebration of Divine Feminine Principles
Goddess Durga's Attributes

- **Strength and Resilience**: Durga's strength and courage in her battle against Mahishasura represent the spiritual power of resilience and the ability to overcome obstacles in one's life.

- **Nurturing and Protective**: Durga's role as a mother goddess symbolizes nurturing and protective qualities, encouraging devotees to seek her guidance and blessings for their personal and spiritual growth.

6. Creation of Sacred Space
Temple Visits and Puja Rituals

- **Sacred Space**: During Navratri, temples and homes are transformed into sacred spaces for worship. The preparation of altars, the decoration of deities, and the performance of pujas create an environment conducive to spiritual reflection and connection with the divine.

- **Community Worship**: The communal aspect of Navratri fosters a collective spiritual experience where devotees join together in worship, sharing in the divine blessings and spiritual energy of the festival.

7. Symbolic Rebirth and Renewal
Cycle of Life

- **Symbolism of Rebirth:** The nine nights of Navratri symbolize the cyclical nature of life, including creation, preservation, and dissolution. The festival encourages devotees to embrace personal transformation and spiritual renewal.

- **Spiritual Rebirth:** Just as the goddess Durga destroys evil and restores balance, the festival inspires devotees to shed past limitations and emerge spiritually renewed.

8. Community and Collective Spirituality
Shared Devotion

- **Community Involvement:** Navratri strengthens community bonds through shared rituals, cultural events, and collective prayers. This communal aspect helps foster a sense of unity and shared spiritual purpose.

- **Collective Aspirations:** The festival is a time for collective aspirations towards spiritual enlightenment and the achievement of common goals of virtue and righteousness.

9. Celebration of the Divine Feminine's Role
Historical Context

- **Historical Significance:** Historically, the veneration of the divine feminine has been central to Hindu spiritual practices. Navratri's focus on Durga underscores the importance of feminine principles in the spiritual hierarchy.

- **Feminine Divine Archetypes**: The festival celebrates the various archetypes of the feminine divine, from the fierce warrior Durga to the nurturing mother Mahagauri, highlighting the diverse roles of the divine feminine in spiritual life.

10. Spiritual Teachings and Philosophical Insights
Philosophical Dimensions

- **Teachings of the Goddess**: The stories and hymns associated with Navratri convey philosophical teachings about the nature of the divine, the nature of reality, and the path to spiritual enlightenment.

- **Philosophy of Balance**: Navratri's themes of balance between good and evil, the interplay of cosmic forces, and the cyclical nature of existence offer deep philosophical insights into the nature of the universe and the human condition.

Conclusion

Navratri's spiritual significance encompasses a wide range of practices, teachings, and beliefs that contribute to personal and communal spiritual growth. The festival serves as a time for devotion, reflection, and renewal, celebrating the divine feminine energy and its role in the cosmic order. Through its rituals, stories, and practices, Navratri offers a profound spiritual experience that inspires both personal transformation and collective spirituality.

The Nine Days of Navratri In Detail

Day 1 of Navratri: Shailaputri

On the first day of Navratri, devotees worship **Shailaputri**, the daughter of the mountains. This day marks the beginning of the nine-night festival dedicated to the goddess Durga. Here's an in-depth exploration of Shailaputri's significance, rituals, and story:

1. Significance of Shailaputri
Symbolism and Attributes

- **Divine Representation**: Shailaputri means "Daughter of the Mountain" (Shaila = Mountain, Putri = Daughter). She is a manifestation of **Parvati**, the wife of Lord Shiva, and represents the nurturing and powerful aspect of the divine feminine energy.

- **Mount Meru**: Shailaputri is associated with **Mount Meru**, considered the center of the physical, metaphysical, and spiritual universe in Hindu cosmology. This mountain symbolizes the stability and strength of the goddess.

- **Symbol of Purity and Devotion**: Shailaputri embodies **purity**, **devotion**, and **spiritual discipline**. Her worship on the first day sets the tone for the rest of the Navratri festival, emphasizing the importance of purity in thought and action.

- **Cosmic Balance**: She represents the balance between the spiritual and material worlds, and her presence signifies the harmony between nature and divinity.

2. Rituals on Day 1
Daily Rituals

- **Preparation for Worship**:
Cleanliness: Devotees start the day by taking a ritual bath and wearing clean, preferably new clothes. Cleanliness is both

physical and spiritual, preparing the devotee for the sacred rituals of the day.

- **Setting Up the Altar:**
Altar Arrangement: An altar or puja area is set up with an image or idol of Shailaputri. The space is decorated with flowers, lamps, and sacred symbols.

- **Invocation of Shailaputri:**
Lighting a Lamp: A diya (lamp) is lit, symbolizing the light of divine consciousness. It is placed in front of the goddess's image or idol.

Offering Flowers and Fruits: Fresh flowers, fruits, and sweets are offered to Shailaputri as symbols of respect and devotion.

- **Recitation of Mantras and Hymns:**
Mantra Chanting: Devotees recite the **Shailaputri Ashtakshara Mantra:**
"ॐ देवी शैलपुत्र्यै नमः" (*Om Devi Shailaputryai Namah*) – "Salutations to the Goddess Shailaputri."

Hymns: Hymns like the **"Shailaputri Stotra"** or verses from the **Devi Mahatmya** are recited to invoke the goddess's blessings.

- **Puja Offerings:**
Aarati: An aarti (ritual of waving a lighted lamp) is performed while singing devotional songs or hymns.

Prayers: Devotees offer personal prayers, asking for strength, purity, and spiritual progress.

- **Fasting:**
Dietary Observances: Many devotees observe a fast, which might include consuming only fruits, milk, and non-cereal-based

foods. Fasting is a way to purify the body and focus the mind on spiritual practices.

Traditional Practices

- **Visiting Temples**: Devotees visit temples dedicated to Shailaputri or Durga to perform the rituals and seek her blessings.

- **Community Gatherings**: Temples and community centers often hold special prayers and gatherings where devotees come together to perform collective worship and participate in devotional activities.

3. The Story of Shailaputri
Mythological Background
Birth and Early Life

- **Daughter of the Himalayas**: Shailaputri is the daughter of the **Himalayan king**, Himavan, and his queen **Mena**. She was born into a royal family of the mountains and is thus associated with the mountain deity.

Marriage to Shiva

- **Union with Shiva**: In her previous birth, she was the daughter of King Himavan and was known as **Sati**. After her marriage to Lord Shiva, she was reborn as Parvati, the daughter of the mountain king.

- **Sati's Self-Sacrifice**: Sati was known for her deep devotion to Shiva, but she was reborn as Parvati to rejoin him after Sati's self-immolation due to her father's insult of Shiva.

Spiritual Significance of Marriage:

- Shailaputri's marriage to Shiva represents the union of the divine feminine and masculine principles. It symbolizes the spiritual completeness and balance achieved through devotion and love.

Early Worship and Devotion

- **Devotion to Shiva**: Shailaputri (as Parvati) is known for her unwavering devotion to Lord Shiva. Her dedication to her husband and her role as the divine consort is celebrated during Navratri, especially on the first day.

- **Role in Cosmic Balance**: Her story reflects the theme of cosmic balance, as she harmonizes the forces of creation and preservation through her divine union with Shiva.

Popular Legends

- **Story of Sati**: One popular legend recounts Sati's previous life where she self-immolated at her father's sacrifice, leading to the creation of Shailaputri as a new form of Parvati to reunite with Shiva.

- **The Return of Durga**: Shailaputri's story is seen as the beginning of the divine journey that culminates in Durga's victory over Mahishasura, symbolizing the spiritual progress from humility and devotion to strength and victory.

Illustrative Images and Icons

- **Iconography**: Shailaputri is depicted riding a bull and holding a lotus and a trident. Her bull represents her connection to the natural world, while the lotus symbolizes purity and the trident signifies her power over the three realms (earth, atmosphere, and heaven).

Visual Representation:

- **Statue or Image**: Shailaputri is often shown with a serene expression, symbolizing her peaceful and nurturing nature.

- **Ritual Implements**: The image of Shailaputri might include sacred symbols like a crescent moon on her forehead and a bull as her vehicle.

4. Devotional Practices and Offerings
Practice
Description

- **Mantra Recitation**: Chanting the Shailaputri Ashtakshara Mantra for divine blessings.

- **Aarti**: Performing aarti with a lighted lamp while singing devotional hymns.

- **Puja Offerings**: Offering flowers, fruits, and sweets to the goddess.

- **Fasting**: Observing a diet of fruits, milk, and simple foods.

- **Temple Visits**: Attending special temple ceremonies and participating in collective prayers.

- **Community Feasts**: Sharing prasad (sacred food) with the community.

5. Spiritual Lessons from Shailaputri

- **Strength Through Devotion**: Shailaputri teaches that spiritual strength and stability are achieved through devotion and purity of heart.

- **The Power of Perseverance**: Her life story exemplifies how perseverance and devotion lead to the ultimate union with the divine.

- **Embracing Purity**: The festival encourages devotees to cleanse themselves spiritually and prepare for a deeper connection with the divine.

Conclusion

Day 1 of Navratri dedicated to **Shailaputri** marks the beginning of a profound spiritual journey. The worship of Shailaputri embodies the virtues of purity, devotion, and strength, setting a foundation for the spiritual practices of the remaining days of Navratri. Through rituals, prayers, and the retelling of her story, devotees seek to align themselves with divine energies and prepare for spiritual growth.

Day 2 of Navratri: Brahmacharini

On the second day of Navratri, devotees worship **Brahmacharini**, one of the nine forms of the goddess Durga. This day emphasizes the qualities of asceticism, devotion, and spiritual discipline. Here's a comprehensive overview of the significance, rituals, and story of Brahmacharini:

1. Significance of Brahmacharini
Symbolism and Attributes

- **Divine Representation**: Brahmacharini means "The One Who Practices Brahmacharya" (Brahma = Creation, Charini = One Who Follows). She represents **self-discipline**, **asceticism**, and **spiritual pursuit**. The term **Brahmacharya** signifies celibacy and dedication to spiritual practices.

- **Symbol of Devotion and Piety**: Brahmacharini embodies the virtues of **devotion**, **purity**, and **sacrifice**. Her worship encourages devotees to practice spiritual discipline and to seek enlightenment through sincere devotion.

- **Goddess of Wisdom and Enlightenment**: As a form of Durga, Brahmacharini symbolizes the pursuit of wisdom and the path to spiritual enlightenment. She teaches the importance of austerity and single-minded dedication to spiritual goals.

Iconography

- **Appearance**: Brahmacharini is depicted as a serene and beautiful young woman dressed in white. She carries a **japa mala** (rosary) in her right hand and a **kamandalu** (holy water pitcher) in her left hand.

- **White Clothing**: Her white attire represents purity and simplicity.

- **Japa Mala**: Symbolizes meditation, prayer, and the repetition of divine names.

- **Kamandalu**: Represents asceticism, spiritual knowledge, and the renunciation of worldly pleasures.

Emblems

- **Crescent Moon**: A crescent moon on her forehead signifies calmness and spiritual purity.

- **Lotus Flower**: Sometimes she is shown with a lotus, which represents divine beauty and spiritual blossoming.

2. Rituals on Day 2
Daily Rituals

1. **Preparation for Worship**:
   Cleanliness: Devotees start by taking a ritual bath and wearing clean clothes, emphasizing physical and spiritual purity.

2. **Setting Up the Altar**:
   Altar Arrangement: An altar or puja area is prepared with an image or idol of Brahmacharini. The space is decorated with flowers, white cloth, and sacred symbols.

3. **Invocation of Brahmacharini**:
   Lighting a Lamp: A diya (lamp) is lit, symbolizing the divine light of knowledge and enlightenment.

   Offering Flowers and Fruits: Fresh flowers, fruits, and sweets are offered to Brahmacharini as symbols of devotion and respect.

4. **Recitation of Mantras and Hymns**:
   Mantra Chanting: Devotees recite the **Brahmacharini Ashtakshara Mantra**:

"ॐ देवी ब्रह्मचारिण्यै नमः:" (*Om Devi Brahmacharinyai Namah*) – "Salutations to the Goddess Brahmacharini."

Hymns: Hymns like the **"Brahmacharini Stotra"** or verses from the **Devi Mahatmya** are recited to invoke her blessings.

5. **Puja Offerings**:
    Aarti: Perform the aarti ritual with a lighted lamp while singing devotional songs dedicated to Brahmacharini.

    Prayers: Offer personal prayers for spiritual growth, wisdom, and the ability to adhere to the path of devotion.

6. **Fasting**:
    Dietary Observances: Devotees may observe a fast, which often includes consuming fruits, milk, and simple foods. Fasting is a way to cultivate self-discipline and focus on spiritual practices.

Traditional Practices

- **Visiting Temples**: Devotees visit temples dedicated to Brahmacharini or Durga to perform the rituals and seek her blessings.

- **Community Gatherings**: Temples and community centers might organize special prayers, devotional singing, and discussions about Brahmacharini's virtues and teachings.

3. The Story of Brahmacharini
Mythological Background
Early Life and Devotion

- **Sati's Rebirth**: Brahmacharini is a manifestation of **Sati** or **Parvati**, the daughter of King Himavan and Queen Mena. In her previous life, she was **Sati**, who was reborn as **Parvati** to fulfill her divine mission of reuniting with Lord Shiva.

Ascetic Practices

- **Austerity for Shiva**: As Parvati, she undertook severe austerities and ascetic practices to win Shiva's love and approval. Her unwavering devotion and rigorous penance symbolize the essence of Brahmacharya.

- **Meditation and Vows**: She observed long periods of meditation and followed strict vows, renouncing all earthly pleasures to achieve her goal.

Story of Brahmacharini's Penance:

- **Commitment to Shiva**: To attain Lord Shiva's favor and be his consort, Parvati practiced **Brahmacharya** (celibacy and dedication) for thousands of years. She engaged in deep meditation and performed intense penance in the Himalayas.

Rewards of Devotion:

- **Blessings from Shiva**: Impressed by her devotion and discipline, Lord Shiva accepted her as his wife, symbolizing the culmination of her spiritual quest and the fulfillment of her divine mission.

Spiritual Meaning

- **Symbol of Self-Discipline**: The story of Brahmacharini emphasizes the power of dedication and self-discipline in achieving spiritual goals. Her life teaches that true devotion requires sacrifice and perseverance.

- **Spiritual Victory**: Brahmacharini's success in winning Shiva's love through her penance represents the triumph of spiritual purity and devotion over the material world.

Popular Legends

- **Legend of the Brahmacharini's Vows**: The legend of Brahmacharini's vow highlights the importance of spiritual discipline and the idea that the divine rewards sincere and dedicated devotion.

- **Parvati's Long Penance**: The story of Parvati's penance reflects the ancient belief in the power of ascetic practices and the idea that spiritual achievements come through disciplined efforts.

Illustrative Images and Icons
Iconography

- **Appearance**: Brahmacharini is usually depicted as a young woman with a serene expression, dressed in white and holding a japa mala and kamandalu.

- **Visual Representation**: She is shown with a crescent moon on her forehead, symbolizing her purity and devotion.

Ritual Implements

- **Japa Mala**: Represents meditation and the recitation of mantras.

- **Kamandalu**: Symbolizes the spiritual knowledge acquired through ascetic practices.

4.Spiritual Lessons from Brahmacharini

- **Path of Discipline**: Brahmacharini's story teaches that spiritual progress requires discipline, self-control, and a focused mind.

- **The Power of Devotion**: Her life exemplifies that sincere devotion to a higher goal leads to spiritual fulfillment and divine blessings.

- **Importance of Purity**: Her worship emphasizes the value of purity in thought, word, and action as essential for spiritual advancement.

Conclusion

Day 2 of Navratri, dedicated to **Brahmacharini**, focuses on the virtues of asceticism, devotion, and spiritual discipline. Her worship encourages devotees to practice purity, devotion, and self-control in their spiritual journeys. Through the rituals, mantras, and the retelling of Brahmacharini's story, devotees are inspired to pursue spiritual goals with dedication and sincerity.

Day 3 of Navratri: Chandraghanta

On the third day of Navratri, devotees worship **Chandraghanta**, a fierce and benevolent form of the goddess Durga. This day focuses on the goddess's qualities of courage, protection, and the power to remove obstacles. Here's a detailed overview of the significance, rituals, and story of Chandraghanta:

1. Significance of Chandraghanta
Symbolism and Attributes

- **Divine Representation: Chandraghanta** means "The One with the Moon on Her Forehead" (Chandra = Moon, Ghanta = Bell). She symbolizes **strength**, **courage**, and **protection**. Her name signifies her divine presence and the auspicious energy she brings to her devotees.

- **Symbol of Strength and Fearlessness:** Chandraghanta embodies the divine feminine's ability to combat evil and protect the righteous. Her worship on the third day signifies the power of divine strength and the importance of fearlessness in the face of challenges.

- **Goddess of Triumph Over Adversity:** She represents the triumph of good over evil and the destruction of obstacles and negative forces. Her form is associated with fighting against demonic forces and ensuring justice and protection for her devotees.

Iconography

- **Appearance:** Chandraghanta is depicted as a beautiful goddess with a serene yet fierce expression. She is adorned with a **crescent moon** on her forehead and a **bell** that symbolizes the call to remove obstacles and bring peace.

Emblems

- **Crescent Moon:** The moon on her forehead signifies calmness, purity, and the cyclical nature of time.

- **Bell:** Represents the ringing of divine power and the removal of fear and obstacles.

- **Weapons**: She holds a variety of weapons in her ten hands, symbolizing her readiness to fight evil forces and protect her devotees.

- **Attire**: She is often shown wearing red or orange clothing, representing her fiery energy and the auspicious nature of the festival.

2. Rituals on Day 3
Daily Rituals

1. **Preparation for Worship:**
   Cleanliness: Devotees begin the day by taking a ritual bath and donning clean clothes, symbolizing the start of a new spiritual endeavor.

2. **Setting Up the Altar:**
   Altar Arrangement: An altar or puja area is set up with an image or idol of Chandraghanta. The space is decorated with flowers, a bell, and sacred symbols.

3. **Invocation of Chandraghanta:**
   Lighting a Lamp: A diya (lamp) is lit, signifying the light of divine presence and the power of the goddess.

   Offering Flowers and Fruits: Devotees offer red flowers, fruits, and sweets as symbols of devotion and respect.

4. **Recitation of Mantras and Hymns:**
   Mantra Chanting: Devotees recite the **Chandraghanta Ashtakshara Mantra**:
   "ॐ देवी चंद्रघंटायै नमः" (*Om Devi Chandraghantayai Namah*) – "Salutations to the Goddess Chandraghanta."

Hymns: Hymns like the **"Chandraghanta Stotra"** or verses from the **Devi Mahatmya** are recited to invoke the goddess's blessings.

5. **Puja Offerings**:
    Aarti: Perform the aarti ritual with a lighted lamp while singing devotional songs dedicated to Chandraghanta.

    Prayers: Offer personal prayers for courage, protection, and the removal of obstacles from one's life.

6. **Fasting**:
    Dietary Observances: Devotees might observe a fast, which often includes consuming fruits, milk, and simple foods. Fasting is seen as a way to purify oneself and focus on spiritual practices.

Traditional Practices

- **Visiting Temples**: Devotees visit temples dedicated to Chandraghanta or Durga for special prayers and rituals.

- **Community Gatherings**: Temples and community centers may organize special pujas, devotional singing, and discussions about Chandraghanta's virtues and powers.

3. The Story of Chandraghanta
Mythological Background
Role in the Divine Cosmic Battle

- **Chandraghanta's Form**: Chandraghanta is a fierce manifestation of Durga who appeared to fight against the demon **Mahishasura**. Her form symbolizes both the gentle and fierce aspects of the goddess, combining beauty with the readiness for battle.

- **Appearance and Preparation**: When Mahishasura's tyranny threatened the gods, they sought the help of Durga. In response, Durga took on the form of Chandraghanta to battle the demon and his forces.

The Battle Against Mahishasura

- **Confrontation with Mahishasura**: Chandraghanta fought bravely against the demon Mahishasura, who was known for his strength and ability to transform into various forms. The bell on her forehead signified the divine call to battle and the promise of victory.

- **Divine Weapons**: Armed with weapons given to her by various gods, she fought Mahishasura and his minions with great valor. Her bell and crescent moon were symbols of her divine authority and the forces of good.
- **Victory Over Evil**: Chandraghanta's battle against Mahishasura represents the triumph of virtue over evil. Her victory assured the protection of the cosmic order and the establishment of peace and justice in the universe.

Popular Legends

- **Legend of the Moon and the Bell**: According to legend, the crescent moon on her forehead represents the promise of divine protection, while the bell signifies the ringing of divine power to remove obstacles and herald success.

- **Story of Mahishasura's Defeat**: The story of Mahishasura's defeat illustrates how the divine feminine energy combats and overcomes evil forces to restore balance in the world.

Illustrative Images and Icons
Iconography

- **Appearance**: Chandraghanta is shown with a serene yet determined expression, with the moon and bell as her prominent symbols.

- **Weapons**: She holds various weapons in her hands, symbolizing her readiness to fight against evil.

Ritual Implements:

- **Bell**: Represents the divine sound that calls to righteousness.

- **Crescent Moon**: Signifies purity and the divine nature of time.

4. Spiritual Lessons from Chandraghanta

- **Strength in Adversity**: Chandraghanta's form teaches that strength and courage are essential in overcoming obstacles and facing challenges in life.

- **The Power of Divine Intervention**: Her story illustrates that divine forces work to restore cosmic balance and ensure the triumph of good over evil.

- **Fearlessness and Protection**: Worshiping Chandraghanta helps devotees seek protection from harm and fear, and it encourages them to face difficulties with bravery.

Conclusion

Day 3 of Navratri, dedicated to **Chandraghanta**, highlights the goddess's role as a fierce protector and a symbol of divine strength. Through her worship, devotees seek courage, protection, and the removal of obstacles in their lives. The rituals, mantras, and stories associated with Chandraghanta emphasize the power of divine intervention and the importance of facing adversities with strength and faith.

Day 4 of Navratri: Kushmanda

On the fourth day of Navratri, devotees worship **Kushmanda**, the fourth form of Goddess Durga. This day celebrates the divine energy of creation and abundance that Kushmanda represents. Here's an in-depth look at her significance, rituals, and story.

1. Significance of Kushmanda
Symbolism and Attributes

- **Divine Representation**: Kushmanda translates to "The Pumpkin Goddess" (Kush = Pumpkin, Anda = Egg). She symbolizes **creation**, **abundance**, and the **cosmic energy** that sustains the universe.

- **Goddess of Creation and Nourishment**: Kushmanda is believed to have created the universe from her **smile**, and she is associated with the **nourishment** and **support** of all creation.

She represents the energy that sustains the universe and provides for all beings.

- **Symbol of Light and Cosmic Energy**: Her presence brings light and joy to the world. She is associated with the power of the sun, which is vital for growth and prosperity.

Iconography

- **Appearance**: Kushmanda is depicted as a beautiful goddess with a radiant smile and a graceful demeanor. She is shown riding a **tiger**, holding a variety of weapons and symbols of prosperity.

Emblems

- **Pumpkin**: Often held in one of her hands, the pumpkin symbolizes abundance, fertility, and the fruit of her creation.

- **Weapons**: She holds several weapons in her ten hands, symbolizing her power to protect and create.

- **Tiger**: Represents her strength and ability to overcome obstacles.

- **Sun**: Sometimes depicted with the sun or radiant aura around her, representing light and energy.

- **Attire**: She is usually adorned in bright, vibrant colors like red or yellow, symbolizing energy, enthusiasm, and prosperity.

2. Rituals on Day 4
Daily Rituals

1. **Preparation for Worship:**
   Cleanliness: Devotees start the day with a ritual bath and wear

clean clothes to prepare for the puja.

2. **Setting Up the Altar:**
Altar Arrangement: The altar is decorated with an image or idol of Kushmanda. It is adorned with flowers, a pumpkin, and other sacred symbols.

3. **Invocation of Kushmanda:**
Lighting a Lamp: A diya (lamp) is lit to symbolize the divine light and the goddess's energy.

Offering Flowers and Fruits: Fresh flowers, fruits, and sweets are offered to Kushmanda as a gesture of devotion and gratitude.

4. **Recitation of Mantras and Hymns:**
Mantra Chanting: Devotees recite the **Kushmanda Ashtakshara Mantra:**
"ॐ देवी कूष्माण्डायै नमः:" (*Om Devi Kushmandayai Namah*) – "Salutations to the Goddess Kushmanda."

Hymns: Hymns such as the **"Kushmanda Stotra"** and verses from the **Devi Mahatmya** are recited to invoke her blessings.

5. **Puja Offerings:**
Aarti: Perform the aarti ritual with a lighted lamp while singing hymns dedicated to Kushmanda.

Prayers: Offer prayers for prosperity, good health, and spiritual growth.

6. **Fasting:**
Dietary Observances: Devotees may observe a fast, which usually includes eating fruits, milk, and simple foods. Fasting helps in spiritual purification and devotion.

Traditional Practices

- **Visiting Temples**: Devotees visit temples dedicated to Kushmanda or Durga for special prayers and rituals on this day.

- **Community Gatherings**:Temples and community centers might organize special pujas, devotional singing, and discussions about Kushmanda's virtues and role in creation.

3. The Story of Kushmanda
Mythological Background
Role in Creation

- **Creation of the Universe**: According to mythology, Kushmanda is believed to have created the universe with her **smile**. Her divine energy brought life and light to the cosmos.

- **The Cosmic Egg**: She is also associated with the **cosmic egg** (Brahmanda), from which the universe was born. This egg symbolizes the beginning of creation and the infinite potential of the universe.

- **The Sun's Energy**: Kushmanda is linked to the **sun** and is considered a source of cosmic energy. She is believed to have harnessed the sun's power to create and sustain the universe.

- **Divine Radiance**: Her smile is said to have been the source of light and creation in the universe, bringing warmth and growth.

The Legend of Kushmanda's Divine Act

- **The Creation of the Cosmos**: As per legends, when the universe was in chaos, the goddess created the world by smiling, bringing order, light, and stability to the cosmos.

- **Role of the Pumpkin**: The pumpkin (kushmanda) is a symbol of abundance and prosperity. It is said that Kushmanda created the world and provided sustenance through the fruits of her labor, symbolized by the pumpkin.

- **Nurturing the Universe**: Kushmanda's role is also to **nurture** and **sustain** all living beings. She is seen as the cosmic mother who provides for the universe and ensures the balance of natural forces.

Popular Legends

- **Legend of the Cosmic Smile**: One popular legend states that Kushmanda's smile was so radiant that it filled the universe with light, transforming the primordial chaos into a structured and orderly cosmos.

- **The Story of the Pumpkin**: The pumpkin is said to represent her ability to provide sustenance and abundance to all creation, symbolizing the fruits of her divine act of creation.

Illustrative Images and Icons
Iconography

- **Appearance**: Kushmanda is depicted with a smiling face, radiant aura, and a pumpkin.

- **Tiger**: She rides a tiger, symbolizing strength and the ability to overcome obstacles.

- **Sun and Light**: Often shown with a glowing aura or the sun, representing her divine energy.

Ritual Implements

- **Pumpkin**: Represents creation, nourishment, and abundance.

- **Sun**: Symbolizes cosmic energy and life-giving force.

4. Spiritual Lessons from Kushmanda

- **Creation and Abundance**: Kushmanda's form teaches that the act of creation brings both the material and spiritual abundance necessary for the universe and all living beings.

- **Cosmic Sustenance**: Her worship reminds devotees of the importance of nurturing and sustaining life, reflecting the divine care that supports the universe.

- **Joy and Light**: The goddess's smile and the light she brings symbolize the joy and positivity that comes from divine grace and the power of creation.

Conclusion

Day 4 of Navratri, dedicated to **Kushmanda**, emphasizes the goddess's role as the creator and nurturer of the universe. Through her worship, devotees seek blessings for creation, prosperity, and spiritual growth. The rituals, mantras, and stories associated with Kushmanda highlight her divine role in bringing light, order, and abundance to the cosmos.

Day 5 of Navratri: Skandamata

On the fifth day of Navratri, devotees worship **Skandamata**, the fifth form of Goddess Durga. This day honors the divine mother who embodies maternal strength and protection. Here's an in-depth look at the significance, rituals, and story of Skandamata.

1. Significance of Skandamata
Symbolism and Attributes

- **Divine Representation:** Skandamata translates to "The Mother of Skanda" (Skanda = Kartikeya, Mata = Mother). She represents **maternal love, protection**, and **strength**.

- **Goddess of Motherhood and Protection**: Skandamata is revered as a motherly figure who embodies the nurturing and protective aspects of the divine feminine. She is the mother of **Kartikeya**, the warrior god, and symbolizes the power of maternal care and support.

- **Symbol of Spiritual Strength**: She represents the strength of a mother who supports and guides her children. Her worship emphasizes the importance of compassion, strength, and the nurturing role of motherhood.

Iconography

- **Appearance**: Skandamata is depicted as a serene and beautiful goddess holding her son, **Kartikeya**, on her lap. She is usually shown seated on a **lotus** and has a calm, loving expression.

- **Emblems: Skanda (Kartikeya)**: Held in her lap, symbolizing the divine son who leads armies and protects the universe.

- **Lotus**: She sits on a lotus, representing purity, divine beauty, and spiritual realization.

- **Four Hands**: She holds a **lotus** in one hand, a **bell** or **axe** in another, and the other two hands are in gestures of blessing and protection.

- **Lion**: Often depicted with a lion as her mount, symbolizing courage and strength.

- **Attire**: She is dressed in bright colors like red or orange, symbolizing vitality, auspiciousness, and spiritual energy.

2. Rituals on Day 5
Daily Rituals

1. **Preparation for Worship:**
   Cleanliness: Devotees start the day by taking a ritual bath and wearing clean clothes, preparing themselves for the puja.

2. **Setting Up the Altar:**
   Altar Arrangement: An altar or puja space is set up with an image or idol of Skandamata. The space is decorated with flowers, a lotus, and other sacred symbols.

3. **Invocation of Skandamata:**
   Lighting a Lamp: A diya (lamp) is lit, symbolizing the divine light and presence of the goddess.

   Offering Flowers and Fruits: Red flowers, fruits, and sweets are offered to Skandamata as a gesture of devotion and respect.

4. **Recitation of Mantras and Hymns:**
   Mantra Chanting: Devotees recite the **Skandamata Ashtakshara Mantra:**
   "ॐ देवी स्कन्दमातायै नमः:" (*Om Devi Skandamatayai Namah*) – "Salutations to the Goddess Skandamata."

   Hymns: Hymns such as the **"Skandamata Stotra"** and verses from the **Devi Mahatmya** are recited to invoke her blessings.

5. **Puja Offerings:**
   Aarti: Perform the aarti ritual with a lighted lamp while singing hymns dedicated to Skandamata.

   Prayers: Offer personal prayers for maternal blessings, protection, and spiritual strength.

6. **Fasting**:
   Dietary Observances: Devotees may observe a fast, often consuming fruits, milk, and simple foods. Fasting is seen as a way to purify oneself and enhance spiritual practices.

Traditional Practices

- **Visiting Temples**: Devotees visit temples dedicated to Skandamata or Durga for special prayers and rituals.

- **Community Gatherings**: Temples and community centers may organize special pujas, devotional singing, and discussions about Skandamata's virtues and maternal qualities.

3. The Story of Skandamata
Mythological Background
Role as the Mother of Kartikeya

- **Birth of Skanda (Kartikeya)**: Skandamata is known as the mother of **Kartikeya**, the war god who leads the divine army against demonic forces. According to legends, she gave birth to Kartikeya after the gods prayed to her for a champion to defeat the demon **Tarakasura**.

- **The Cosmic Battle**: Kartikeya, guided and nurtured by Skandamata, played a crucial role in defeating Tarakasura and restoring cosmic order. Skandamata's role as his mother signifies her support in his divine mission.

- **The Nurturing Mother**: Skandamata's depiction with Kartikeya highlights the divine strength and guidance that a mother provides to her child, symbolizing her nurturing role in the universe.

The Legend of Skandamata's Divine Acts

- **Support for Kartikeya**: The legend narrates how Skandamata nurtured Kartikeya, who was destined to lead the gods in battle against the demons. Her strength and care ensured his success in the divine battle.

- **Symbol of Divine Motherhood**: Skandamata represents the ideal qualities of a mother—love, protection, and strength. Her story teaches about the significance of maternal care in achieving success and overcoming challenges.

Popular Legends

- **Legend of the Divine Birth**: According to the legend, when the demon Tarakasura was causing havoc in the heavens, the gods realized that only a divine warrior could defeat him. They prayed to Skandamata, who then gave birth to Kartikeya to lead the celestial army.

- **The Story of Kartikeya's Victory**: Kartikeya's victory over Tarakasura was a pivotal event in the mythological battles between the forces of good and evil. Skandamata's support was crucial in this victory, symbolizing her role as a divine protector.

Illustrative Images and Icons
Iconography

- **Appearance**: Skandamata is shown with a peaceful and loving expression, holding Kartikeya in her lap.

- **Lotus**: Symbolizes purity and spiritual growth.

- **Lion**: Represents courage and strength.

Ritual Implements

- **Lotus**: Represents purity and divine beauty.

- **Kartikeya**: Symbolizes divine strength and leadership.

4. Spiritual Lessons from Skandamata

- **Strength in Maternal Care**: Skandamata's form teaches the power and importance of maternal care and the divine strength that comes from nurturing and protecting loved ones.

- **Support and Guidance**: Her story emphasizes the role of a mother as a guide and protector, offering support and strength to help overcome challenges.

- **Spiritual Growth Through Devotion**:Worshiping Skandamata helps devotees seek spiritual growth and divine blessings through the virtues of love, protection, and strength.

Conclusion

Day 5 of Navratri, dedicated to **Skandamata**, focuses on the goddess's role as a nurturing and protective mother. Through her worship, devotees seek maternal blessings, spiritual strength, and protection. The rituals, mantras, and stories associated with Skandamata highlight her divine role in creation, protection, and the nurturing of divine heroes.

Day 6 of Navratri: Katyayani

On the sixth day of Navratri, devotees honor **Katyayani**, the sixth form of Goddess Durga. This day is dedicated to the goddess who embodies **valor** and **victory** over evil. Here's a comprehensive exploration of her significance, rituals, and story.

1. Significance of Katyayani
Symbolism and Attributes

- **Divine Representation**: Katyayani translates to "The Daughter of Sage Katyayana" (Katyayani = Daughter of Katyayana). She is revered as a fierce and powerful form of Durga, symbolizing **courage, victory**, and the **destruction of evil**.

- **Goddess of Valor and Justice**: Katyayani is known for her role as a warrior goddess who fights against the forces of darkness and injustice. Her worship is associated with seeking **victory** and **overcoming obstacles**.

- **Symbol of Divine Strength**: She embodies the strength and righteousness needed to combat evil and protect the righteous. Her form and attributes emphasize divine intervention and the triumph of good over evil.

Iconography

- **Appearance**: Katyayani is depicted as a fierce and radiant goddess, often shown with a powerful, commanding presence. She has a warrior-like demeanor and an assertive posture.

Emblems

- **Lion**: She rides a lion, symbolizing **strength, courage**, and the ability to overcome obstacles.

- **Weapons**: She holds a variety of weapons like a **sword, trident**, and **bow**. These symbolize her role as a fierce warrior and protector.

- **Lotus**: A symbol of purity and spiritual growth, often seen in her hands or as part of her vehicle.

- **Four Hands**: Typically, she holds a **sword** in one hand, a **lotus** in another, a **trident** or **axe** in a third hand, and gives blessings or protection with the fourth.

- **Attire**: She is dressed in vibrant colors like **red** or **orange**, representing **strength**, **courage**, and the power to destroy evil.

2. Rituals on Day 6
Daily Rituals

1. **Preparation for Worship**:
   Cleanliness: Devotees start the day with a ritual bath and wear clean clothes to prepare for the puja.

2. **Setting Up the Altar**:
   Altar Arrangement: An altar is set up with an image or idol of Katyayani. The space is decorated with flowers, a lion symbol, and other sacred symbols.

3. **Invocation of Katyayani**:
   Lighting a Lamp: A diya (lamp) is lit to symbolize the divine light and presence of the goddess.

   Offering Flowers and Fruits: Red flowers, fruits, and sweets are offered to Katyayani as a gesture of devotion and respect.

4. **Recitation of Mantras and Hymns**:
   Mantra Chanting: Devotees recite the **Katyayani Ashtakshara Mantra**:
   "ॐ देवी कात्यायन्यै नमः" (*Om Devi Katyayani Namah*) – "Salutations to the Goddess Katyayani."

   Hymns: Hymns such as the **"Katyayani Stotra"** and verses from the **Devi Mahatmya** are recited to seek her blessings.

5. **Puja Offerings:**
   Aarti: Perform the aarti ritual with a lighted lamp while singing hymns dedicated to Katyayani.

   Prayers: Offer personal prayers for victory, strength, and overcoming challenges.

6. **Fasting:**
   Dietary Observances: Devotees may observe a fast, consuming fruits, milk, and simple foods. Fasting helps in spiritual purification and devotion.

Traditional Practices

- **Visiting Temples:** Devotees visit temples dedicated to Katyayani or Durga for special prayers and rituals on this day.

- **Community Gatherings:** Temples and community centers may organize special pujas, devotional singing, and discussions about Katyayani's virtues and role as a warrior goddess.

3. The Story of Katyayani
Mythological Background
Birth and Role

- **Birth of Katyayani:** Katyayani was born as the daughter of **Sage Katyayana**. Her birth was the result of the sage's intense penance to receive a daughter who would have the strength to vanquish the demons.

- **Defeating Mahishasura:** Katyayani is often depicted as the goddess who fought and defeated the demon **Mahishasura**, who was causing havoc in the heavens and on earth. She assumed this form to restore cosmic order.

- **Victory Over Evil**: In the legend, Mahishasura, a demon with the ability to change forms, had terrorized the gods and was unchallenged. Katyayani took the form of a fierce warrior to fight him, symbolizing the divine force needed to overcome great evil.

The Legend of Katyayani's Divine Acts

- **The Battle with Mahishasura**: The gods, distressed by Mahishasura's tyranny, sought help from Katyayani. She fought a fierce battle with the demon, showcasing her strength and courage. With her divine weapons and the support of the gods, she defeated Mahishasura and restored peace.

- **Symbol of Righteous War**: Katyayani's victory represents the triumph of good over evil through righteousness and divine intervention. Her battle was not just a physical fight but also a spiritual one, symbolizing the struggle for justice and righteousness.

Popular Legends

- **The Legend of the Battle:** The story of Katyayani's battle with Mahishasura is a central mythological event that highlights her role as a fierce protector of the righteous and destroyer of evil.

- **The Blessing of Sage Katyayana:** Sage Katyayana's penance for a divine daughter is also a significant aspect of her legend, emphasizing the power of devotion and righteousness in invoking divine grace.

Illustrative Images and Icons
Iconography

- **Appearance**: Katyayani is shown with a fierce and determined expression, holding weapons and riding a lion.

- **Lion**: Symbolizes her strength and courage.

- **Weapons**: Sword, trident, and lotus represent her warrior prowess and spiritual wisdom.

Ritual Implements

- **Lion**: Represents courage and strength.

- **Weapons**: Symbolize divine power and protection.

- **Lotus**: Represents spiritual purity and enlightenment.

4.Spiritual Lessons from Katyayani

- **Courage and Valor**: Katyayani's form teaches the importance of courage and valor in facing challenges and fighting against injustice.

- **Divine Intervention**: Her story emphasizes the role of divine forces in restoring balance and righteousness in the world.

- **Strength Through Devotion**: Worshiping Katyayani helps devotees cultivate inner strength and seek divine support in their battles against personal and external adversities.

Conclusion

Day 6 of Navratri, dedicated to **Katyayani**, focuses on the goddess's role as a fierce and courageous warrior. Through her worship, devotees seek blessings for victory, strength, and the overcoming of obstacles. The rituals, mantras, and stories associated with Katyayani highlight her divine role in fighting evil and protecting the righteous.

Day 7 of Navratri: Kalaratri

On the seventh day of Navratri, devotees worship **Kalaratri**, the seventh form of Goddess Durga. This day is dedicated to the fierce and transformative aspect of the goddess. Here's a detailed look at the significance, rituals, and story of Kalaratri.

1. Significance of Kalaratri
Symbolism and Attributes

- **Divine Representation: Kalaratri** translates to "The Dark Night" (Kala = Dark, Ratri = Night). She is known as the **fierce form of Durga** who embodies the **destruction of ignorance** and the **overcoming of darkness**.

- **Goddess of Destruction and Transformation**: Kalaratri is revered as the destroyer of evil forces and obstacles. Her form represents **transformation, endings,** and the **unveiling of truth** through the destruction of ignorance and falsehood.

- **Symbol of Divine Wrath**: She is a form of Durga that exhibits divine wrath against those who oppose righteousness and justice. Her fierce appearance signifies the power to destroy evil and protect the devotees.

Iconography

- **Appearance**: Kalaratri is depicted as a fearsome and dark-skinned goddess with a **terrifying** yet **protective** demeanor. Her appearance contrasts sharply with the other forms of Durga.

Emblems

- **Dark Skin**: Her dark complexion symbolizes the **power to remove ignorance** and darkness from the world.

- **Messy Hair**: Her disheveled hair represents her fierce and untamed nature.

- **Weapons**: She holds a **sword**, a **trident**, and often has a **noose** and a **mace**. These symbolize her ability to destroy evil and protect the righteous.

- **Mount**: She is often depicted riding a **donkey**, which symbolizes **humility** and the **destruction of pride**.

- **Attire**: She wears **dark, simple attire**, signifying her fierce nature and the process of destruction as a step towards transformation.

2. Rituals on Day 7
Daily Rituals

1. **Preparation for Worship:**
    Cleanliness: Devotees start the day with a ritual bath and wear clean clothes to prepare for the puja.

2. **Setting Up the Altar:**
    Altar Arrangement: An altar is set up with an image or idol of Kalaratri. The space is decorated with **black** or **dark-colored** flowers and symbols of destruction.

3. **Invocation of Kalaratri:**
    Lighting a Lamp: A diya (lamp) is lit to symbolize the divine light and presence of the goddess.

    Offering Flowers and Fruits: Black or dark-colored flowers, fruits, and sweets are offered to Kalaratri as a gesture of devotion and respect.

4. **Recitation of Mantras and Hymns:**
    Mantra Chanting: Devotees recite the **Kalaratri Ashtakshara Mantra:**
    "ॐ देवी कालरात्र्रि नमः:" (*Om Devi Kalaratri Namah*) – "Salutations to the Goddess Kalaratri."

    Hymns: Hymns such as the **"Kalaratri Stotra"** and verses from the **Devi Mahatmya** are recited to invoke her blessings.

5. **Puja Offerings:**
    Aarti: Perform the aarti ritual with a lighted lamp while singing hymns dedicated to Kalaratri.

    Prayers: Offer personal prayers for overcoming fears, obstacles, and the destruction of negative influences.

6. **Fasting**:
   Dietary Observances: Devotees may observe a fast, consuming fruits, milk, and simple foods. Fasting is seen as a way to purify oneself and enhance spiritual practices.

Traditional Practices

- **Visiting Temples**: Devotees visit temples dedicated to Kalaratri or Durga for special prayers and rituals.

- **Community Gatherings**: Temples and community centers may organize special pujas, devotional singing, and discussions about Kalaratri's role as a fierce destroyer of evil.

3. The Story of Kalaratri
Mythological Background
Role as the Destroyer of Demons

- **The Form of Kalaratri**: Kalaratri is a fierce form of Durga that appears during the intense battle against evil forces. She assumes this form to confront and destroy powerful demons and restore cosmic order.

- **Defeating the Demons**: In the legend, Kalaratri played a crucial role in the **battle against the demon duoSumbha** and **Nishumbha**, who were terrorizing the gods and the universe. Her fierce form was necessary to vanquish these powerful demons.

The Legend of Kalaratri's Divine Acts

- **The Battle with Sumbha and Nishumbha**: According to the myth, when the demons Sumbha and Nishumbha attacked the heavens and defeated the gods, they created havoc. The gods sought the help of Kalaratri, who took on the terrifying form to fight the demons. Kalaratri's fierce appearance and weapons helped her defeat the demons, symbolizing the divine power required to overcome great evil.

- **Symbol of Destruction Leading to New Beginnings**: Kalaratri's role as a destroyer reflects the principle that destruction is a necessary step for creation and transformation. Her fierce form represents the ultimate force that dismantles the old to make way for the new.

Popular Legends

- **The Legend of the Demons**: The story of Kalaratri's battle against Sumbha and Nishumbha is central to her legend. She is invoked to destroy overwhelming evils that cannot be defeated by conventional means.

- **The Fierce Form of Durga**: Kalaratri's fierce form contrasts with other forms of Durga and signifies the transformative power of destruction in the cosmic order.

Illustrative Images and Icons
Iconography

- **Appearance**: Kalaratri is shown with a dark complexion, disheveled hair, and a fierce expression.

- **Weapons**: Sword, trident, and noose symbolize her role in destruction and protection.

- **Mount**: The donkey symbolizes humility and the destruction of pride.

Ritual Implements

- **Dark Flowers**: Symbolize the power to overcome ignorance and darkness.

- **Weapons**: Represent divine force and the destruction of evil.

4. Spiritual Lessons from Kalaratri

- **Embracing Transformation**: Kalaratri's form teaches the importance of embracing change and transformation as part of spiritual growth.

- **Overcoming Ignorance**: Her story emphasizes that true progress involves confronting and destroying ignorance and falsehood.

- **Divine Intervention in Times of Crisis**: Worshiping Kalaratri helps devotees seek divine support in overcoming major challenges and adversities.

Conclusion

Day 7 of Navratri, dedicated to **Kalaratri**, focuses on the goddess's fierce form as the destroyer of evil and ignorance. Through her worship, devotees seek blessings for overcoming fears, obstacles, and the darkness of ignorance. The rituals, mantras, and stories associated with Kalaratri highlight her role in the cosmic battle between good and evil, and her power to bring about transformation.

Day 8 of Navratri: Mahagauri

On the eighth day of Navratri, devotees worship **Mahagauri**, the eighth form of Goddess Durga. This day is dedicated to the goddess who represents **purity**, **peace**, and **spiritual elevation**. Here's a detailed look at the significance, rituals, and story of Mahagauri.

1. Significance of Mahagauri
Symbolism and Attributes

- **Divine Representation**: Mahagauri translates to "The Great White Goddess" (Maha = Great, Gauri = White). She is celebrated as the embodiment of **purity**, **serenity**, and **spiritual grace**.

- **Goddess of Purity and Peace**: Mahagauri is known for her pure and peaceful nature. Her worship is associated with seeking **spiritual upliftment**, **purification of the soul**, and the attainment of **inner peace**.

- **Symbol of Divine Grace**: Her form signifies the transformation of divine energy into a state of grace and beauty. She represents the ultimate state of spiritual perfection and divine love.

Iconography

- **Appearance**: Mahagauri is depicted as a beautiful goddess with a **white** or **fair** complexion. Her serene and calm demeanor reflects her role as a source of peace and purity.

Emblems:

- **White Complexion**: Symbolizes purity, peace, and divine grace.

- **Four Hands**: She holds a **trident** (trishul), a **drum** (damaru), and a **lotus** in her hands, and the fourth hand is in a gesture of **blessing**.

- **Mount**: She rides a **bull**, symbolizing **dharma** (righteousness) and **strength**.

- **Attire**: She is adorned in **white or light-colored attire**, signifying her pure and serene nature.

2. Rituals on Day 8
Daily Rituals

1. **Preparation for Worship:**
   Cleanliness: Devotees start the day with a ritual bath and wear clean, light-colored clothes to prepare for the puja.

2. **Setting Up the Altar:**
Altar Arrangement: An altar is set up with an image or idol of Mahagauri. The space is decorated with **white** flowers, **light-colored** fabrics, and symbols of purity.

3. **Invocation of Mahagauri:**
Lighting a Lamp: A diya (lamp) is lit to symbolize the divine light and presence of the goddess.
Offering Flowers and Fruits: White flowers, fruits, and sweets are offered to Mahagauri as a gesture of devotion and respect.

4. **Recitation of Mantras and Hymns:**
Mantra Chanting: Devotees recite the **Mahagauri Ashtakshara Mantra:**
"ॐ देवी महागौरि नमः:" (*Om Devi Mahagauri Namah*) – "Salutations to the Great Goddess Mahagauri."

Hymns: Hymns such as the **"Mahagauri Stotra"** and verses from the **Devi Mahatmya** are recited to invoke her blessings.

5. **Puja Offerings:**
Aarti: Perform the aarti ritual with a lighted lamp while singing hymns dedicated to Mahagauri.

Prayers: Offer personal prayers for spiritual growth, purification, and peace.

6. **Fasting:**
Dietary Observances: Devotees may observe a fast, consuming fruits, milk, and simple foods. Fasting helps in spiritual purification and devotion.

Traditional Practices

- **Visiting Temples**: Devotees visit temples dedicated to Mahagauri or Durga for special prayers and rituals on this day.

- **Community Gatherings**: Temples and community centers may organize special pujas, devotional singing, and discussions about Mahagauri's virtues and role as a symbol of purity and peace.

3. The Story of Mahagauri
Mythological Background
The Form of Mahagauri

- **Transformation of Parvati**: Mahagauri is a form of **Goddess Parvati**, who transformed from her previous fierce forms into a more serene and graceful appearance. This transformation symbolizes the ultimate state of purity and divine beauty.

- **The Legend of Mahagauri's Purification**: According to the legend, Parvati performed intense penance to please Lord Shiva. After enduring hardships and overcoming obstacles, she was blessed by Shiva and took the form of Mahagauri, symbolizing her ultimate spiritual elevation and purity.

The Story of Mahagauri's Divine Acts

- **Penances and Devotion**: Parvati's devotion and penance were aimed at gaining Shiva's love and acceptance. Her transformation into Mahagauri symbolizes the divine grace she received through her steadfast devotion.

- **Symbol of Divine Grace**: In her form as Mahagauri, she represents the ultimate state of grace and spiritual purity. Her worship is a way for devotees to seek divine grace and spiritual enlightenment.

Popular Legends

- **The Legend of Purification**: The story of Mahagauri emphasizes the importance of purification and spiritual practice. It illustrates that through devotion and perseverance, one can attain the highest spiritual state.

- **The Legend of Parvati's Penitence**: The transformation from Parvati to Mahagauri signifies the process of spiritual growth and the grace that follows sincere devotion and penance.

Illustrative Images and Icons
Iconography

- **Appearance**: Mahagauri is depicted with a fair complexion, serene expression, and adorned with beautiful ornaments.

- **Weapons and Symbols**: Trident, drum, lotus, and bull symbolize divine power, righteousness, and purity.

Ritual Implements

- **White Flowers**: Symbolize purity and spiritual elevation.

- **Bull**: Represents righteousness and divine strength.

4. Spiritual Lessons from Mahagauri

- **Pursuit of Purity**: Mahagauri's form teaches the importance of **spiritual purity** and the path to spiritual enlightenment.

- **Grace and Devotion**: Her story emphasizes that through sincere **devotion** and **penance**, one can achieve divine grace and spiritual growth.

- **Peace and Serenity**: Worshiping Mahagauri helps devotees seek **inner peace** and the strength to overcome spiritual obstacles.

Conclusion

Day 8 of Navratri, dedicated to **Mahagauri**, focuses on the goddess's serene and pure form, symbolizing spiritual elevation and grace. Through her worship, devotees seek blessings for purification, spiritual growth, and inner peace. The rituals, mantras, and stories associated with Mahagauri highlight her role as a symbol of purity and divine grace.

Day 9 of Navratri: Siddhidatri

On the ninth and final day of Navratri, devotees worship **Siddhidatri**, the ninth form of Goddess Durga. This day is dedicated to the goddess who embodies **perfection, fulfillment of desires,** and **spiritual accomplishments**. Here's a detailed look at the significance, rituals, and story of Siddhidatri.

1. Significance of Siddhidatri
Symbolism and Attributes

- **Divine Representation**: Siddhidatri translates to "The Bestower of Siddhis" (Siddhi = Spiritual Perfection, Datri = Giver). She is revered as the goddess who grants **spiritual powers**, **perfections**, and **accomplishments** to her devotees.

- **Goddess of Fulfillment and Accomplishment**: Siddhidatri is worshiped for attaining **siddhis** (spiritual powers) and achieving the highest forms of **spiritual success**. She embodies the **completion of spiritual quests** and the fulfillment of divine wishes.

- **Symbol of Divine Perfection**: Her form represents the culmination of all spiritual endeavors, embodying the perfection of both the material and spiritual realms.

Iconography

- **Appearance**: Siddhidatri is depicted with a **serene** and **radiant** appearance, symbolizing her role as the bestower of spiritual and material fulfillment.

Emblems

- **Four Hands**: She holds a **lotus** (symbolizing purity and divine beauty), a **mace** (representing spiritual authority), a **discus** (symbolizing the power to destroy evil), and a **rosary** (symbolizing meditation and spiritual practice).

- **Mount**: She is often depicted seated on a **tiger**, symbolizing her supreme power and the ability to conquer all obstacles.

- **Attire:** She is adorned in **bright** and **radiant** attire, often in **red or golden colors**, symbolizing the divine energy and power she bestows upon her devotees.

2. Rituals on Day 9
Daily Rituals

1. **Preparation for Worship:**
   Cleanliness: Devotees begin the day with a ritual bath and wear clean clothes to prepare for the puja.

2. **Setting Up the Altar:**
   Altar Arrangement: An altar is set up with an image or idol of Siddhidatri. The space is decorated with **bright colors** and **flowers,** particularly **lotus flowers.**

3. **Invocation of Siddhidatri:**
   Lighting a Lamp: A diya (lamp) is lit to represent the divine light and presence of the goddess.

   Offering Flowers and Fruits: Bright flowers, fruits, and sweets are offered to Siddhidatri as a gesture of devotion and respect.

4. **Recitation of Mantras and Hymns:**
   Mantra Chanting: Devotees recite the **Siddhidatri Ashtakshara Mantra:**
   "ॐ देवी सद्धिधदात्री नमः:" (*Om Devi Siddhidatri Namah*) – "Salutations to the Goddess Siddhidatri."

   Hymns: Hymns such as the **"Siddhidatri Stotra"** and verses from the **Devi Mahatmya** are recited to invoke her blessings.

5. **Puja Offerings:**
   Aarti: Perform the aarti ritual with a lighted lamp while singing hymns dedicated to Siddhidatri.

Prayers: Offer personal prayers for the attainment of spiritual powers, success in endeavors, and fulfillment of divine wishes.

6. **Fasting**:
Dietary Observances: Devotees may observe a fast, consuming fruits, milk, and simple foods. Fasting helps in spiritual purification and devotion.

Traditional Practices

- **Visiting Temples**: Devotees visit temples dedicated to Siddhidatri or Durga for special prayers and rituals on this day.

- **Community Gatherings**: Temples and community centers may organize special pujas, devotional singing, and discussions about Siddhidatri's role in granting spiritual powers and fulfillment of desires.

3. The Story of Siddhidatri
Mythological Background
The Form of Siddhidatri

- **Role in the Cosmic Order**: Siddhidatri is considered the embodiment of all the **siddhis** (spiritual powers) in the universe. Her form is associated with the ultimate spiritual achievement and the fulfillment of divine purposes.

The Story of Siddhidatri's Divine Acts

- **Creation of Siddhis**: According to the legend, Siddhidatri is the creator and distributor of all divine powers. She is the source of the **siddhis** that allow sages, saints, and devotees to achieve spiritual enlightenment and success.

- **Blessing of Lord Shiva**: It is said that Siddhidatri bestowed her divine grace upon Lord Shiva, granting him the power to fulfill his cosmic responsibilities. Her blessings helped Shiva in his role as the preserver and destroyer of the universe.

- **The Legend of the Divine Powers**: Siddhidatri's story highlights how she imparts various spiritual powers to her devotees. Through her grace, devotees can attain wisdom, strength, and divine abilities.

Popular Legends

- **The Legend of Siddhis**: One popular legend states that all the gods and goddesses approach Siddhidatri to receive their respective powers. She is revered as the goddess who bestows these siddhis upon those who seek her blessings.

- **The Legend of Siddhidatri's Grace**: The story emphasizes that through sincere worship and devotion, one can receive her grace, which leads to the attainment of spiritual powers and the fulfillment of divine wishes.

Illustrative Images and Icons
Iconography

- **Appearance**: Siddhidatri is shown with a bright complexion, serene expression, and adorned with divine ornaments.

- **Weapons and Symbols**: Lotus, mace, discus, and rosary represent divine grace, spiritual authority, and the powers of meditation and practice.

Ritual Implements:

- **Lotus Flowers:** Symbolize divine beauty and purity.

- **Tiger:** Represents the power to overcome obstacles and achieve spiritual goals.

4. Spiritual Lessons from Siddhidatri

- **Attainment of Spiritual Powers:** Siddhidatri's worship teaches that through divine grace and devotion, one can attain **spiritual powers** and achieve **siddhis.**

- **Fulfillment of Divine Desires:** Her story emphasizes that devotion and faith can lead to the **fulfillment of divine wishes** and the accomplishment of spiritual goals.

- **Completion of Spiritual Endeavors:** Siddhidatri represents the successful culmination of spiritual quests and the attainment of spiritual **perfection.**

Conclusion

Day 9 of Navratri, dedicated to **Siddhidatri,** focuses on the goddess's role as the bestower of spiritual powers and the embodiment of divine fulfillment. Through her worship, devotees seek blessings for spiritual success, the attainment of divine powers, and the fulfillment of their spiritual aspirations. The rituals, mantras, and stories associated with Siddhidatri highlight her role as the ultimate source of divine grace and spiritual accomplishment.

Conclusion: Embracing the Divine Legacy

As we reach the end of this exploration into the divine world of Durga Maa and the sacred festival of Navratras, it is time to reflect on the journey we have undertaken together. We have delved into the origins, stories, and rituals that celebrate the nine powerful forms of the goddess, uncovering the profound significance behind each aspect of the festival.

CHAPTER NINE

Reflection on Navratras

Navratras is not merely a sequence of rituals and traditions; it is a vibrant celebration of the divine feminine energy that resides within all of us. Each day of the festival is a testament to the multifaceted nature of Durga Maa, offering lessons in strength, wisdom, compassion, and resilience. By understanding and participating in these rituals, we connect with the deeper spiritual essence of our culture and draw strength from the stories of the goddess.

CHAPTER TEN

Continuing the Tradition

The preservation and celebration of our cultural heritage are vital in maintaining our identity and passing on the values that have shaped our civilization. As we celebrate Navratras, let us remember the importance of these traditions and ensure that they are cherished and practiced by future generations. Sharing these stories, participating in the rituals, and teaching our children about the significance of Durga Maa are crucial steps in keeping our heritage alive.

CHAPTER ELEVEN

Inspiration for Modern Lives

The teachings and stories of Durga Maa are not confined to the past; they are powerful sources of inspiration for our contemporary lives. As modern women face challenges and strive for success, the goddess's attributes offer valuable lessons in empowerment, balance, and self-respect. By embracing these teachings, we can navigate the complexities of modern life with grace and strength.

CHAPTER TWELVE

A Call to Action

As we conclude this book, I invite you to carry forward the legacy of Durga Maa and Navratras. Embrace the stories, partake in the rituals, and let the divine energy of the goddess guide you in your journey. Celebrate the festival with devotion and understanding, and inspire others to do the same. In doing so, we not only honor our cultural heritage but also enrich our lives with the timeless wisdom and strength of Durga Maa.

May the divine blessings of Durga Maa be with you always, guiding and protecting you on your path. Let us celebrate the power, compassion, and wisdom of the goddess, today and always.

CHAPTER THIRTEEN

Closing Thoughts

Thank you for joining me on this journey through the enchanting world of Durga Maa and Navratras. It is my hope that this book has not only deepened your understanding of these sacred traditions but also inspired you to embrace and celebrate our cultural heritage with renewed fervor. Together, let us keep the spirit of Durga Maa alive, ensuring that her stories and teachings continue to inspire and empower future generations.

CHAPTER FOURTEEN

Durga Chalisa

Salutations to you, O Durga, the bestower of happiness. Salutations
to you, O Amba, the remover of pain.
Your light is formless, illuminating the three worlds.
Your forehead shines like the moon, and your face is large and
magnificent. Your eyes are red, and your brows are fierce.
O Mother, your form is exceedingly charming. Seeing it,
devotees feel great joy.
You have created the world with your power. To sustain it, you
provide food and wealth.
As Annapurna, you nourish the world. You are also the prime
beauty.
At the time of dissolution, you destroy everything. You are
Gauri, the beloved of Shiva Shankar.
Yogis and ascetics sing your praises. Brahma and Vishnu
meditate on you constantly.
You took the form of Saraswati to grant wisdom, rescuing sages
and seers.
You manifested as Narasimha, tearing apart the pillar and
emerging.
You protected Prahlad and sent Hiranyakashipu to heaven.
You took the form of Lakshmi, residing in the body of Shri
Narayan.
In the ocean of milk, you reside, full of compassion, fulfilling
our desires.

In Hinglaj, you are worshipped as Bhavani. Your glory is limitless and indescribable.
You are Matangi and Dhumavati, Bhuvaneshwari and Bagala, bestowing happiness.
As Bhairavi, you protect the world. As Chhinna Bhala, you remove suffering.
You ride a lion, accompanied by the brave Langur.
In your hand, you hold a skull and a sword. Seeing you, even death flees in fear.
You wield weapons and a trident, causing the hearts of enemies to tremble.
You reside in Nagarkot, your fame resounding in the three worlds.
You slew the demons Shumbh and Nishumbh and destroyed the evil Raktabeej and Shankhan.
Mahishasur, the proud king, whose burden troubled the earth, was annihilated by you.
In your fierce form as Kali, you destroyed him with your army.
Whenever saints were in dire distress, you came to their aid, O Mother.
Your glory is revered in the immortal city and the realm of the gods, keeping everyone free from sorrow.
Your light shines in Jwala. Men and women worship you always.
Those who sing your praises with love and devotion will never face suffering or poverty.
Those who meditate on you with a focused mind will be freed from the cycle of birth and death.
Yogis, gods, and sages proclaim that there is no yoga without your power.
Shankar, the great ascetic, achieved perfection through his tapasya, conquering desire and anger, merging into you.
He meditated on Shankar day and night, never once remembering you.
Not understanding the essence of your power, he lamented when it departed.

Seeking refuge, he praised you, chanting, "Victory, victory,
victory to you, O Jagadamba Bhavani."
The primordial mother, pleased, granted power without delay.
O Mother, you have given me great sorrow. If you do not help
me, I have no strength left.
Seeking refuge, Raghunath was saved, bringing the Sudarshan
Chakra in his hand.
When Mahishasur was vanquished, the whole world became
joyous.
Those who meditate on you with a focused mind will not face
birth or death.
Liberation in life is easily attained, and gods, men, and sages all
praise you.
Doha:
O Ashtabhuja, bestower of devotion, you are the protector of
the entire creation.
My saint prays to you constantly. Victory, victory, victory to
you, O Jagadamba Bhavani.

CHAPTER FIFTEEN

Ambe Ji Ki Arti

Om Jai Ambe Gauri, Hail Ambe Gauri, Mother, hail Shyama Gauri. Hari, Brahma, and Shiva constantly meditate on you. Om Jai Ambe Gauri…

Adorned with vermilion on the forehead, with a sandalwood mark. Your eyes are bright, your face is like the moon. Om Jai Ambe Gauri…

Your body is like gold, dressed in red garments. A garland of red flowers adorns your neck. Om Jai Ambe Gauri…

Riding on a lion, wielding a sword and a skull cup. You are served by gods, men, and sages, removing their sorrows. Om Jai Ambe Gauri…

Earrings shine, a pearl on the nose. Your light radiates like millions of moons and suns. Om Jai Ambe Gauri…

You destroyed Shumbh and Nishumbh, slayer of Mahishasur. Your eyes are like smoky lotuses, ever intoxicated. Om Jai Ambe Gauri…

You destroyed Chanda and Munda, destroyed the blood-seed demon. You killed Madhu and Kaitabh, making the gods fearless. Om Jai Ambe Gauri…

You are Brahmani, Rudrani, and the queen of Kamala. The Vedas and scriptures praise you, you are the queen of Shiva. Om Jai Ambe Gauri…

Sixty-four Yoginis sing auspicious songs, Bhairav dances. Drums and cymbals play, the damaru resounds. Om Jai Ambe Gauri…

You are the mother of the world, you are the sustainer. You remove the sorrows of devotees and grant them happiness and prosperity. Om Jai Ambe Gauri...
Your four arms are radiant, holding a sword and a skull cup. Men and women who serve you obtain their desired fruits. Om Jai Ambe Gauri...
In a golden plate, incense and camphor lamps are placed. In Shri Malaketu, your light radiates like millions of jewels. Om Jai Ambe Gauri...
Whoever sings the Aarti of Shri Ambeji, Says Swami Shivanand, will attain happiness and prosperity. Om Jai Ambe Gauri...
Hail Ambe Gauri, Mother, hail Shyama Gauri...

About The Author

An Indian woman with a passion for writing since an early age, I have carved a niche in the literary world as the published author of five Amazon No.1 bestseller books. My writing journey has been diverse, exploring various topics, like poetry (in hindi and english) and relationships but I have found a profound connection in writing about history and mythology.

I often mention it as "history" because I believe this is true not just myth.

My first mythology book on Lord Hanuman,"**The mysteries of Hanuman,**" became a significant hit, resonating with both young minds and adults. It offers a treasure trove of stories and wisdom that inspire and educate. My second mythology book, delving into the fascinating avatars of Lord Vishnu,"**Vishnu's Legacy**" has also garnered popularity for its engaging short stories and insightful knowledge.

A Hindi poetry book, **Waqt ke Pannon Per**, an English poetry book, **Tides of Feelings,** and a heart-touching book on relationships, **Heartstrings**, are among the nuggets of my writings.

Now, I bring to you my third history and mythology book,"**Divine Mother Durga**" focused on Durga Maa and the vibrant festival of Navratras. This book aims to provide comprehensive information about the Navratras and the Navdurga. It explores the rituals and significance of each day, guiding you on how to perform the puja and embrace the spiritual essence of the festival.

With each book, I strive to preserve and celebrate our rich cultural heritage, making it accessible and engaging for all. Join me on this journey of exploration and reverence, and discover the profound stories and practices that have shaped our traditions.